Praise

'It gives me great pleasure, as President of The Tutors' Association, to recommend this book to parents who would like to understand the 11 Plus process and many of the peculiarities of the primary-secondary school transition in the UK.'

— **John Nichols**, President of the Tutors' Association

'An invaluable step-by-step guide to getting you and your child successfully through the 11 Plus.'

— **Annabel from NappyValleyNet**

'Forget the school gate whispers, this book tells you the truth about how to help your child succeed in the 11 Plus.'

— **Clapham Parent**

HOW TO PASS THE
11 PLUS

An insider's guide to schools, tutoring and exam success

MARY LONSDALE

To Sophie and Jamie, my own 11 Plus guinea pigs, and a huge thank you to Maddie for working so hard with me on the creation of this book.

R^ethink

First published in Great Britain in 2022 by Rethink Press
(www.rethinkpress.com)

© Copyright Mary Lonsdale

Contents

Foreword

The transition from primary to secondary school is a period of great anxiety for many parents. It is only entirely natural that parents will be concerned that their child makes the transition into an appropriate school that will offer them the opportunity to flourish, develop and be guided through the next stage of their educational careers. Many parents will recognise that the choice of secondary school has the potential to shape a student's trajectory – indeed, their own child, not just any student. It is also true that secondary schools have a different but transformative influence over one's life direction compared to primary schools.

It is against this backdrop that *How to Pass the 11 Plus* has been written. This book by Mary Lonsdale highlights the importance of calm and rational thinking and the careful consideration of different options for each child. It is well-researched and provides a fantastic opportunity for parents to learn about the process of transition, including not only how to prepare for the famous 11 Plus exam, but also what to consider when choosing a school and how to compare different sources of information that are available. It provides impartial, objective details of how 11 Plus examinations are set, practical advice on how to prepare for them, and realistic guidance on the factors to consider when selecting a secondary school.

It gives me great pleasure as President of The Tutors' Association to recommend this book to parents who would like to understand the 11 Plus process and many of the peculiarities of the primary-secondary school transition in the UK. Whilst the UK has one of the most highly regarded school systems in the world (especially amongst selective schools), like the UK's constitutional arrangements, it has evolved gradually over many years (indeed, centuries) and can be complex and daunting for the uninformed. Any effort to provide better guidance to parents on how this process works and how they can do the best for their child is welcome.

Regardless of where your child ends up going to school, whether they receive additional support or not, and how well they perform in the 11 Plus, the fact that you, as a parent, take a keen interest in their education and provide them with the guidance, discipline and good counsel they need will be invaluable to them. This book will certainly help you to understand this step on their educational journey but no book can solve all problems. You and your children are human and imperfect; there will be setbacks on the way. However, a well-considered approach will certainly be best for your child and know that if you are positive, consistent, firm and encouraging you are doing the best that you can for them. Work hard and reap the rewards of your efforts.

John Nichols
President of The Tutors' Association

Introduction

Today, my memories of sitting the 11 Plus are largely impressionistic: the cold air outside the building, my growing nervousness and fluttering insides, the hunt for where I was to sit, the intensity of the exam, and the relief when it was done. I doubt I am alone in this.

Most of my friends at primary school had not applied for the 11 Plus; it was not the normal path for a girl from south Liverpool in the 1980s. The isolation of the process added additional uncertainty: what was I doing? And for what end? My family had no tradition of public schooling; however, my mum and dad were both teachers. They were determined I should go to a school that could develop my passion for English and reading. And so, they assumed the task of preparing me for the big day.

They did well. As soon as the invigilator told us to turn over our papers in the crowded exam room, the work I had done paid off in a furious rush of writing and calculating. Afterwards, my mum eagerly asked me how it went. To her annoyance, I could barely remember.

When the results arrived, we all rushed down to stare at the letter waiting in my mother's hands. It was rather fat. A good sign, surely? She opened it up: 'We are pleased to be able to offer you a place at Merchant Taylors' School for Girls...' I did not realise it at the time, but I had just successfully navigated one of life's major forks in the road. I remember the wave of relief and my mum's fierce hug, then going to choose my Raleigh Chopper bike as a reward. This is the moment I want for your child too.

Thirty years later, I run one of the most established tutoring agencies in Britain: Mentor Education. *School Report* independently rated us as London's number one tuition agency, and we also feature in *The Good Schools Guide*. Thousands of pupils have come through our doors and gone on to thrive at amazing schools.

I still get that rush of joy when a child succeeds but I see around me many parents who let the time for making the right choices slip past them. Too many parents at the school gate who say 'what will be will be' – only to find that there are few options left for their child. Too many parents who say 'they will end up in the right school for them' – only to find that their bright child did not get into the right school for them, when they absolutely should have. Too many parents who say 'school will prepare them' – only to find their child has not been taught the curriculum for the 11 Plus exam.

The truth is that the 11 Plus process, whether for grammar or independent schools, is a one-off opportunity. Grab it and your child can be at a school that will harness their abilities, inspire them and maximise their performance at GCSE and A Level. Miss it and, worst-case scenario, your child could end up playing catch-up for the rest of their school career. Yet this critical moment in your child's life is surrounded by mystique born of an implicit competition. Parents whisper about tutors at the school gate, scour forums and hoard information hoping to gain an advantage and spread gossip as if it were gospel.

This book is our attempt to dispel the fog of misinformation, to give you the knowledge that you need to make the best choices for your children, and to be your personal guide on the 11 Plus journey.

We start with a simplified guide to the 11 Plus: its various components, the different types of assessment your child might encounter and a brief history of its place in the UK school system.

The type of 11 Plus assessment that your child will face depends on the schools they are applying to, and therefore choosing the right school for your child is a crucial aspect of the 11 Plus process. There are various factors that play into this decision, and I have included a detailed guide to help you identify an appropriate set of target schools for your child and to break down the admissions process.

Once you have selected a number of target schools, the key question that every parent wants to know about the 11 Plus assessment is how to pass it. In the chapter 'Exam Subjects in Detail' (Chapter 5), we dive into each component of the exams – English, Maths, Verbal Reasoning and Non-verbal Reasoning – and advise you on how you can prepare your child for success in each area. Next, I lay out a clear and proven strategy based on a twelve-month timeline, which helps your child to peak as the exam season approaches. I explain how to develop good exam technique, as well as how to make learning fun for your child. I also go into detail on the importance of mock exams, emphasise the crucial role that reading plays in 11 Plus success, and give practical tips on staying calm on exam day itself.

Interviews are not used by every school as part of their 11 Plus assessment, but if you choose to apply for an independent school, it is likely to be a key element of the process. In Chapter 8, I provide a practical guide to preparing your child for the interview stage, including how to support shy children. I also include information and advice on online interviews and provide a list of common interview questions. Group interviews and assessments are increasingly used by selective schools in addition to or as a variation of the interview. As such, I have included a section on this type of assessment.

Next, it is time to discuss the 't' word: tutoring. Tutoring is the great but silent arms race of the 11 Plus. At certain schools, there are inevitably more applicants than places. Many parents wish to maximise the chances of their child achieving entry to their first-choice school. That is where tutoring comes in. Chapter 9, 'The Role of Tuition', will help you to decide when and if your child needs a tutor, what you should look for in a tutor, how intensely you should tutor and what kind of tutoring options are available. I also explain how the industry works so that you can get the most out of tuition if you choose to go down this route.

For many parents, getting a scholarship to an independent school is the holy grail of the 11 Plus process. This is a significant achievement, and a standard approach to passing the exam will rarely line up your child for the scholarship options available at their target schools. Our chapter on scholarships (Chapter 10) details how to prepare for both academic and non-academic scholarships, and how to maximise your child's chances of success. I also offer information on applying to school bursaries.

The 11 Plus process can undoubtedly be stressful for both children and families. However, to give your child the best chance of success it is important to reduce their anxiety and support their emotional and physical wellbeing throughout this period. It is also vital to manage your own emotions, as placing excessive pressure on children can backfire when it comes to academic achievement. Our chapter on wellbeing (Chapter 11) will explain why emotional and physical health is so important and provide practical tips on how to support your child throughout the 11 Plus process. I also offer tips on reducing stress within the family, and on preparing for results day.

The 11 Plus journey does not end with the examination. Parents often come to the team at Mentor for advice on accepting offers and dealing with waiting lists, so we've included a chapter on what happens next (Chapter 12). Unfortunately, not every 11 Plus journey is successful, but there are options available to you as a parent, either to appeal the decision or to find an alternative option. I explain what these are and detail how you can access them in case you need to.

After the long admissions process, everyone wants their child to have the best start to their Year 7 journey. In our final chapter, 'Starting Secondary School', I offer essential advice to help ensure that your child's experience at secondary school is a positive one.

The 11 Plus can be a daunting experience. It requires a considerable amount of work for both you and your child and, like all important events, it can place a good deal of pressure on those involved. But it is worth it. Achieving a place at the right school is an amazing accomplishment and will benefit your child, not only for the duration of their time there, but for the rest of their life. Putting in the necessary effort now, working hard and, crucially, working correctly, can save you hours of heartache in the future.

The 11 Plus is by no means the biggest challenge your child will face, but it will likely be the first. While you cannot eliminate the stressful aspects of the process, through preparation and planning you can minimise them. This book aims to do just that. At Mentor Education, we provide hundreds of families each year with advice on choosing schools, assessing academic potential, and preparing for the 11 Plus process through tuition, mock exams, interview practice and more. In this book, I hope to distil the expertise I have gathered over four decades in the industry into an easy-to-read and accessible format that will help your family tackle the 11 Plus with confidence, clarity and calm.

You and your child have a journey to make, and this book can be your guide. Good luck!

PART ONE
CHOOSING TO TAKE THE 11 PLUS

The decision to put your child in for the 11 Plus will have far-reaching consequences for them, you and all the family; it should not be taken without research and consideration. In the next chapters we explain the history of the 11 Plus, break down the typical elements of the exam itself, and update you on recent developments in 11 Plus assessments, to help you decide whether preparation for this assessment would be a good idea for your child.

ONE

Understanding The 11 Plus

Simply put, the 11 Plus is an assessment process undertaken by students hoping to gain entry to selective schools (including independent schools, grammar schools and some other state schools). The 11 Plus is usually taken by students during the Autumn term or early January of Year 6, but this will depend on the schools your child is applying to.

The type of assessment that your child will face is also dependent on their choice of school, and in this chapter, I offer more information on the different types of assessment your child might encounter. Generally, an 11 Plus written examination will include papers on English, Maths, Verbal Reasoning and Non-verbal Reasoning. It may also include an interview, a group activity and a reference provided by your child's current school. Later in the book, I will go into each of these elements in more detail and guide you through the preparation your child will need.

Some particularly competitive schools also set 'pre-tests' to reduce the number of candidates that will complete the later application stages. I'll provide more information on the pre-test later in this chapter.

History of the 11 Plus

Historically, fee-paying schools had an entrance system called the Common Entrance, which was taken by pupils aged twelve or thirteen. The state system had a different approach, which was to select children at eleven. After the educational reforms of the 1940s and the introduction of grammar schools, children took an examination in what we now call Year 6 to determine whether they would go to a grammar school or a secondary modern. This examination was the original iteration of what we now call the 11 Plus.

The 11 Plus system (for grammar schools) and the 13 Plus system (for independents) existed alongside one another for decades. But for various reasons, such as the phasing out of grammar schools in the late 1990s, independent schools also began to introduce entrance at 11 Plus, necessitating the development of their own 11 Plus entrance process. Today, most day schools tend to use 11 Plus as their primary entrance point, while many of the older boarding schools maintain 13 Plus as their primary entry point.

The upshot of these historic changes is that, while fifty years ago the 11 Plus was essentially a state school entry system, today it is predominantly used by independent schools (as well as a few remaining grammar schools).

The organic growth of the 11 Plus means that it is not centrally coordinated by the various schools that use it, and many have developed their own specific tests. Many educational providers, such as GL, CEM and Atom, also produce assessments that schools can use. Each provider's examinations will have variations in approach and emphasis, and this is why it is helpful to know which schools your child will be applying to before you begin the process of 11 Plus preparations. This chapter provides information on some of the differences between the papers provided by each of these boards.

Components of 11 Plus written examinations

The 11 Plus examinations taken by students between September and January of Year 6 usually consist of up to four components:

- Maths
- English
- Verbal Reasoning
- Non-verbal Reasoning

Chapter 5, 'Exam Subjects in Detail', will provide more detail on each element and how best to prepare for it.

It is important to note that, unlike English and Maths, Verbal and Non-verbal reasoning are not part of the national curriculum. If your child attends a prep school, they will be given some in-school preparation for reasoning exams, but if they are at a state primary, they will not. In this scenario, it is even more essential that your child does as much preparation as possible for the examination. This is where external tuition can be particularly valuable. See our chapter on 'The Role of Tuition' (Chapter 9) for advice on deciding whether your child would benefit from tuition.

Examination boards

Most independent and grammar schools base their 11 Plus assessments on exam papers written by two organisations: CEM and GL Assessment. An organisation called ISEB also increasingly provides assessments for schools' 11 Plus process, in partnership with GL. These assessments are known as the ISEB Pre-Test. It is important that you do not confuse the ISEB Pre-Test with the type of 'pre-test' that some schools ask children to take to cut down the number of candidates who take their full 11 Plus assessment – although to add to the confusion, some schools do use the ISEB as part of this early-stage assessment. We will clarify the difference between these two 'pre-tests' later in the chapter.

It is important to find out which type of assessment your child's target school prefers to use, as CEM, GL and the ISEB Digital Pre-Test differ in significant ways. It is also helpful to have this information because there are specialist resources available to help your child prepare for the type of exam they are sitting. Check the admissions section on the websites of your target schools: these usually contain information about the board that administers their exams, as well as familiarisation materials that will help you find out other crucial information, such as the format of the exam, the timing, the interview process, and so on.

GL Assessment

The exam papers produced by GL Assessment are used by most grammar schools for their entrance examinations. GL, which stands for Granada Learning, is an independent assessment business, who have developed a wide range of assessments with the help of partners including King's College London and the University of York. GL are also responsible for developing the ISEB Digital Pre-Test, so preparation for the assessments produced by GL are useful for the ISEB, and vice versa. See below for more information on the ISEB Digital Pre-Test.

The papers produced by GL for the 11 Plus consist of four separate papers for English, Maths, Non-verbal Reasoning and Verbal Reasoning. In some cases, depending on their selection criteria, schools will opt to not use all four papers for their entrance assessments. There are two formats for the GL Assessment – either standard format or multiple-choice – and the papers tend to be approximately forty-five minutes long.

GL Assessment questions are all drawn from a question bank of 13,000 questions, which means that practice is rewarded. There is a distinct set of question types for each paper, and the format is reproduced yearly with only minor differences, so careful preparation means that a child can comfortably be ready for the exam. GL offers ten hours of free familiarisation material, as well as the option to pay for practice packs in whichever subject or subjects are needed.

CEM assessments

CEM stands for the Centre for Evaluation & Monitoring, previously part of the University of Durham, now part of the University of Cambridge. CEM assessments were created in response to fears from some schools that the existing 11 Plus exams had become too easy to prepare for, particularly with the help of tuition. To this end, CEM do not produce or endorse any published practice papers and continually change the format of the tests. The CEM test is used as the basis for the written examinations of most independent schools in England. It is generally considered to be more difficult than the GL, and increasingly grammar schools are also opting to use CEM because of this perception.

Although each school requests that their 11 Plus tests are individualised, all CEM assessments share attributes which can be practised and improved. Although CEM do not publish any practice papers themselves, well-regarded providers of exam preparation resources such as Bond do offer practice papers that are tailored to CEM. It is certainly not the case that it is 'impossible' to prepare for the test.

The ISEB Digital Pre-Test

The ISEB stands for the Independent Schools Examinations Board. This is the examining body that has for many years set the 11+ and 13+ Common Entrance exams for various boarding schools.

More recently, the ISEB and GL developed a pre-test for 13 Plus applicants to take in Year 6 or Year 7. This is used by boarding schools to predict if a child is likely to meet their academic standard one or two years in advance of a child potentially joining their school at thirteen. If a child passes the pre-test, they will usually be offered an unconditional place at a school, or a place contingent on them achieving a certain grade at their Common Entrance exam at thirteen. Many boarding schools enthusiastically adopted the Common Pre-Test because it allowed them to make offers to children in Year 6, when good candidates might also be receiving attractive 11 Plus offers from other secondary schools.

Due to covid-19, normal entrance exams could not go ahead in 2020. Schools urgently needed a tried-and-tested digital option. For the most part, they adopted the ISEB Common Pre-Test as an alternative to their normal written papers. A key advantage of the ISEB test is that children only had to sit one exam and the results were then distributed to all schools they had applied for. This was felt by many to be a vast improvement on the multiple exams children normally sit for the 11 Plus. It also meant that teachers did not have to mark thousands of papers to assess candidates and were instead given a pre-marked score. Some schools have decided to continue using the ISEB Digital Pre-Test as their 11 Plus assessment, or more commonly as one part of it. As ever, check the admissions page of your target schools' websites to clarify what types of assessment your child will need to sit.

Key things to know about the ISEB Digital Pre-Test:

- The ISEB Digital Pre-Test consists of tests in Mathematics, English, Verbal Reasoning and Non-verbal Reasoning.

- All questions are multiple-choice.

- All questions are compulsory, and children cannot go back once a question has been answered.

- The tests take about two and a half hours to complete, with different amounts of time allocated to different sections.

- The tests are adaptive, meaning the questions get easier or more difficult depending on the performance of the candidate. This is designed to give a more accurate reading of the candidate's ability because questions that are too easy do not always allow high-performing candidates to demonstrate their full potential.

- There is a progress bar to show candidates how far through the questions they are and a timer to show the time remaining.

- Candidates are allowed a pencil and paper for working out during the Verbal Reasoning and Mathematics tests, but not during the Non-verbal Reasoning or English tests.

- ISEB does not endorse any practice tests produced by other companies. However, there is a familiarisation test available on their website.

- Examples and practice questions, where relevant, are provided during the tests so that candidates understand what is being asked of them.

The ISEB Pre-Test has a similar syllabus to other 11 Plus entrance exams and it is provided by GL. To some extent, therefore, students can prepare as they would for traditional written exams with GL. But there are some specific aspects of exam technique that your child will need to develop to do well in digital tests. See our chapter on 'Exam Technique' (Chapter 6) for more information on how to prepare your child for success in the Digital ISEB and other types of digital examination.

Pre-tests

Some oversubscribed schools make a first cut of candidates using a 'pre-test' in the autumn of Year 6. Again, this is not necessarily the same as the ISEB Pre-Test discussed above, though it may be for some. Any pre-test functions to identify children who are unlikely to reach the academic standards required to thrive at the school. Typically, schools will cut half of applicants at this point, which makes marking the full examination papers that successful candidates take later in the year a far more realistic prospect for staff.

Pre-tests can trip parents and students up because they take place earlier than the full examination (from September to November rather than January). If the schools your child is applying to use pre-tests then it is important to factor this into your planning as your child will need to be prepared for examinations earlier than most.

Pre-tests are usually digital examinations that analyse reasoning skills (both verbal and non-verbal). Although some claim that reasoning assessments test children's innate abilities and therefore cannot be prepped for, this is simply not true. It is perfectly possible for your child to practise the various permutations of Verbal and Non-verbal Reasoning questions that are likely to crop up, and to improve both their results and – equally importantly – their speed. Pre-tests tend to be very time-pressured, so effective exam technique is vital to ensure your child can get through all the questions. Parents should begin to factor in timed revision practice during the Year 5 summer holidays prior to the pre-test exam. As ever, it is important to check what kind of pre-test your child will be facing, as a digital exam demands different preparation from a written paper.

The 11 Plus process is certainly challenging, but it does not need to be stressful. With the right support, the correct organisational strategies, and a calm approach your child can achieve the results they need and gain entry to the schools of their choice. This book will give you the tools to make the process as smooth as possible and to give your child the best chance of success.

In the next chapter, we discuss why choosing a school for your child is such an important decision, detail some of the factors that should play into your choice and guide you through the admissions process.

TWO

Choosing A School For Your Child

Choosing a secondary school for your child is a hugely important decision that will affect not only their time there, but the rest of their life.

To assist you in making this choice, I have compiled a list of the key considerations you should factor into your decision-making process. None of these choices are necessarily a black-and-white decision but ruling out broad categories can help to make the selection process less daunting. In this chapter, I'll expand on these factors in more detail and take you through the steps involved in making your choice.

As a parent, you should start to research secondary schools in Year 4. There is no need to involve your child in the decision until later in the process, but it can take longer than you might think to narrow down options, so getting a good head start is worth it.

Independent, grammar or non-selective state school?

Independent schools

In the UK, the terms 'independent', 'private' and 'public' school are used interchangeably and refer to fee-paying schools. Independent schools are not controlled by local authorities, and are not required to follow the national curriculum. Students do, however, sit the same exams at GCSE and A Level or International Baccalaureate (IB) as pupils at grammar or state schools, though there may be a wider choice of subjects on offer. There is significant variation between schools, but sending your child to an independent school means they are likely to benefit from factors such as smaller class sizes, more extra-curricular opportunities and better facilities (for activities such as Sport, Drama and Art). There may also be a greater emphasis on academic achievement, although this is also a central focus for many grammar and selective state schools.

The cost of education at an independent school varies significantly, but fees of around £6,000 per term for day schools and £12,000 for boarding schools are typical.

Many of these schools offer full or partial bursaries, and it is well worth researching if any of your target schools offer this. Another option for parents unable to meet the cost of private education is to consider whether your child would be suited to a scholarship application. See the chapter on scholarships (Chapter 10) for more details.

Grammar schools

Grammar schools are, in most cases, state-funded schools that select pupils based on their performance in the 11 Plus assessment process. Today, there are 163 grammar schools in England and a further 69 in Northern Ireland. There are no state grammars in Wales or Scotland.[1]

Before the education reforms of the late 1960s, all children in the UK took an examination at the end of primary school that determined whether they would attend a grammar school, which emphasised academic attainment and sent many students on to higher education, or a secondary modern, designed more for children going into trade professions.

In the late 1960s and 70s, it was felt that the division of children at such a young age based on an assessment

---

1   Shadi Danechi, *Grammar School Statistics* (House of Commons Library, 2020) https://researchbriefings.files.parliament.uk/documents /SN01398/SN01398.pdf, accessed 23 December 2021

was overly simplistic and there was a drive to phase out grammar schools. As a result, comprehensive schools were created with the intention that all children learn together in the same environment.

Some areas and schools resisted this change, and England and Northern Ireland retain several selective grammar schools. Some grammar schools decided to become independent schools rather than comprehensives, meaning that some schools with 'grammar' in their name are actually fee-paying schools (eg Kingston Grammar School). Some areas, including Kent, Essex and Buckinghamshire, resisted the move to comprehensive schools entirely and maintained the grammar school system. The old secondary moderns in these areas are now referred to as non-selective schools. Other areas embraced a hybrid model whereby they only reduced the number of grammar schools.

The benefits of attending a grammar school include:

- **A more academic learning environment:** Because entry to grammar school is based on academic performance in the 11 Plus, students are generally of the same ability. This allows teachers to pitch lessons more effectively than is possible at mixed-ability comprehensive schools.

- **High performance in examinations:** Research suggests that pupils from grammar schools achieve better results at GCSE than pupils from state schools.[2] Grammar schools also consistently perform well in local and national league tables, and often send their pupils on to higher education.

- **Improved life chances and social mobility:** Research suggests that pupils who attend a grammar school will go on to out-earn those who attended a non-selective school.[3]

How do you get into a grammar school? First, it is vital to check whether your child meets the school's criteria. Although grammar schools nominally have an admissions process that allows all students to apply for the school, in practice it is difficult for students outside of the school's catchment area to get in, regardless of their exam performance.

Competition for grammar schools is extremely fierce, and children hoping to gain entry to a grammar school will need to prepare diligently for their 11 Plus assessment.

Non-selective state schools

Non-selective state schools are state-funded schools that students attend without sitting an entrance exam

---

2   Shadi Danechi, *Grammar School Statistics* (2020)
3   Luke Sibieta, 'Can grammar schools improve social mobility?' (Institute for Fiscal Studies, 2016) https://ifs.org.uk/publications /8469, accessed 23 December 2021

based on academic ability. They follow the national curriculum.

The non-selective state school system includes comprehensives, free schools, academies and PRU schools. Free schools are a recent innovation allowing parents or companies to set up schools more easily. Academies are schools free of local authority control and have more freedom to set their own agendas and control their finances. PRU schools are designed to provide education for children who are unable to attend a mainstream school or academy. Pupils are often referred to a PRU if they need a higher level of support than a mainstream school can provide.

Non-selective state schools vary considerably depending on the local authority, the school's particular ethos and the level of funding provided by government. Many non-selective state schools receive excellent results, and it is well worth researching the schools in your area to see if any would be suitable for your child.

Further key considerations for choosing a school

Your child's personality

Most parents considering an independent or grammar school wish their child to attain good exam results and the opportunity to study at a good university. However, there are many different learning environments that can provide these results. Ultimately your child should be at the centre of the decision-making process. Considering their needs and preferences is vital to ensuring they have a positive school experience.

As your child gets to age nine or ten, you will start to get a few clues as to the kind of educational establishments they will be comfortable in. For instance, if they are particularly creative or sporty, will they suit a learning environment that focusses strongly on academic success or one with a more rounded approach? If they are shy, will they suit a big school or a smaller learning environment? Is there a particular subject that they excel in and is the school known for providing good support in that area?

It is also important that the secondary school your child attends reflects your own values as a family, as well as your commitments and lifestyle.

Single-sex or mixed?

There are pros and cons to both single-sex and mixed educational environments and your choice should largely be rooted in your child's preference and personality.

One factor you might want to consider is your child's confidence. Single-sex schools can be great for allowing children to express themselves in ways they might not feel comfortable doing in a mixed environment, whether that is academically, socially or in extra-curricular activities. Studies have shown that girls are more likely to choose traditionally 'male' subjects like Science or Maths at single-sex schools, and boys are more likely to feel comfortable choosing subjects like art, drama, design and food technology. Girls also tend to perform better academically in single-sex environments, and to have more opportunities on the sports field because more resources are made available to them.

There are benefits to mixed environments that you should consider too, such as learning how to socialise with the opposite sex and being exposed to a more diverse range of perspectives and opinions as a student. This is important for preparing for life beyond school and some students do express regret later in life that they did not have more interaction with people of the opposite sex while at school.

It can be useful to talk to the parents of children you know at both mixed and single-sex schools to get a better sense of what might be right for your child. It is also important to remember that the ethos of the school itself will have an impact on how much the make-up of the school affects its students.

Day school or boarding?

For some parents – such as those who live internationally or those not based near the schools of their choice – boarding school is an obvious option. For others, the choice between day schools or boarding is more complicated, and there are various factors you might wish to consider.

If your child is very active or is someone that likes to try lots of extra-curricular activities, then boarding school can be a great option, as they often provide a greater choice of activities and more expansive facilities than day schools. The fact that students live on-site means that pupils often have more time for both academic studies and extra-curricular activities, as they do not have to commute to school. Boarding schools also demand more independence of students, which can be beneficial for some children. Students at boarding schools often form close bonds, which might be an advantage for your child if they do not have siblings or live somewhere very isolated. Do be aware, however, that boarding schools tend to suit children with strong, confident personalities. If your child is shy or anxious, boarding school might not be the best option.

Some children may find starting secondary school without the support of their family around them challenging. Children who struggle to make friends might experience loneliness at boarding school, and if you are not seeing your child regularly it is harder to stay on top of wellbeing issues like this. It is also more difficult to intervene if they experience bullying or are struggling with any other aspect of school. But it is worth noting that some boarding schools are now offering more flexible options, such as weekends at home, which can alleviate some of these issues.

Another factor to consider is that day schools are usually more selective than boarding schools and therefore tend to dominate the academic league tables. Price is also a key consideration: day schools are usually much less expensive per term than boarding schools.

Facilities

The impressive facilities on show at many independent and grammar schools can be very persuasive. It is vital that you keep your child's own interests and passions centre of mind. A school might have a state-of-the-art Science wing, or an Olympic-sized swimming pool, but if your child's passion is for Art or Drama then this is where your attention should be focussed.

Location and commute

One way to narrow down the choice of secondary school for your child is to think about the location. It is important to consider how long your child's commute will be, as having a short and stress-free journey to school is undoubtedly beneficial for students. Most schools would recommend only applying if your commute will be less than an hour.

You might also consider the kind of after-school activities your child may want to participate in. For instance, if they have a club, rehearsal, or sports fixture after school, is it reasonable for them to then travel home in the dark at 6 or 7pm? And will you be able to easily attend any events that the school might be hosting from your workplace or home?

If the school offers a coach service, this will eliminate a lot of stress from your child's journey and provide an opportunity for them to make friends. You might also want to consider schools that would require an active commute such as walking or cycling as this is a healthy start to the day and will guarantee that your child stays active.

Academic performance of the school

There is huge variation in academic performance between schools, even among schools that appear highly comparable. Not all children will suit the most academically focussed schools, whether due to temperament, learning style, ability, or preference. However, if your child is academically motivated, then it is important to consider the performance of the school to give them the best chance of exam success. Take a look at the league tables that are published every year to get a sense of how the schools you are considering perform academically.

Your next question is probably, 'How academic a school is right for my child?' There are various indications that can help you answer this question and ensure that your child makes a set of school applications that strikes the right balance between ambition and realism in terms of their abilities.

One of the most important data points to consider is your child's current academic attainment in relation to their peers. You need to understand this at a level deeper than, say, 'they are third in the class', or 'she got 75% in a Maths test'. You need to understand where your child sits within bigger cohorts such as their national peer group and the peer group for grammar or independent school selective entry. This will give you far more context than the small bubble of a single class or year group.

One way to gather this information is simply to ask your child's teacher or school if they have any data that can show where your child sits on a larger scale. Children are regularly tested at school, so it is likely that there is some useful information that you can gather in this way.

An alternative is for your child to take an academic assessment. These are offered by various educational consultancies, and they are an excellent diagnostic tool for parents looking to gauge their child's academic potential.

The CEM computer-based test (InCAS) is one of the most sophisticated assessments available and, thanks to their large data pool, offers meaningful data regarding your child's abilities relative to their peers. In addition, many independent schools work with CEM to produce their own entrance exams, so these results will provide you with a strong sense of your child's academic strengths and weaknesses.

Entry to high-achieving schools is extremely competitive and requires rigorous preparation. It is therefore crucial to consider your child's character before putting them in the running for these schools. Is this a challenge they are likely to embrace, or might the exam put undue pressure on them? Will the academic pressures of the school itself suit them, or might they better suit somewhere with a different focus?

Equally, you might wish to consider if you as a parent or family are willing to sacrifice the time and commitment necessary to help your child succeed in the 11 Plus. For instance, if your values as a family are strongly linked to relaxation and quality time, will you be willing to sacrifice weekends and holidays? If you enjoy group activities, are you willing to forego time spent together to ensure the required work is done? If you undertake frequent travel or have additional caring responsibilities, you may decide that you simply can't take on the extra workload required by secondary school preparation.

THREE

Researching Your Chosen Schools

Once you have a shortlist of potential schools, you can begin the process of further research from home to build a better picture of each.

Some resources you might wish to consider include:

- OFSTED or ISI (Independent Schools Inspectorate) reports
- League tables
- School websites and prospectuses
- Schools' guides (eg *The Good Schools Guide*)
- Online forums
- Word of mouth

OFSTED or ISI reports

OFSTED stands for the Office for Standards in Education, Children's Services and Skills. It is a UK government body responsible for inspecting all state schools and some independent schools. A different body, the Independent Schools Inspectorate or ISI, inspects the majority of independent schools.

OFSTED reports

The purpose of OFSTED inspections is to assess four key areas:

- Quality of education

- Behaviour and attitudes

- Personal development

- Leadership and management

OFSTED also delivers an overall judgement of school performance on the following scale:

- Outstanding

- Good

- Requires improvement

- Inadequate – falling into one of two categories: serious weaknesses or requiring special measures

Schools rated 'outstanding' were previously exempt from full inspections, but as of 2019 they are also required to have a full inspection on the usual schedule of once every five years. Schools given 'requires improvement' or 'inadequate' are inspected on a more regular basis to check on their progress.

OFSTED reports are useful for parents, as they give a sense of prospective schools' performance and educational approach. Inspectors will gather information about a school ahead of an inspection, but schools are only given one working day's notice, meaning that the reports tend to give a fair and unvarnished view. On inspection day, inspectors will sit in on lessons, observe records and schoolwork, and communicate directly with students, staff, governors and parents. Each OFSTED report is approximately ten pages long and provides a detailed overview of everything from safeguarding to the progress of pupils with SEND.

ISI reports

The ISI is a government-approved body, whose investigations are based on standards set by the government. However, they use different criteria for their reports, designed to reflect the generally higher level of achievement and greater emphasis on extra-curricular activities of the schools they inspect compared to those inspected by OFSTED. The ISI conducts two types of report: educational quality reports and regulatory compliance reports.

The ISI does not give a single judgement on a school, but instead gives a grade for each report, again on a sliding scale:

- Excellent

- Good

- Sound

- Unsatisfactory

Educational quality reports focus on two main criteria: pupils' achievement and their personal development. Reports also consider factors contributing to these outcomes, such as curriculum, teaching, pastoral care, governance, leadership and management. Reports will give an overall grade, a detailed assessment of the school's performance, and a clear sense of how pupils' examination results compare with national benchmarks. Education quality reports are useful for parents, as they give an indication of a school's academic performance, its atmosphere and ethos, and the level of pastoral care available to students.

Regulatory compliance reports simply provide a summary of whether or not the school in question meets the minimum standards required by relevant educational regulations.

Schools undergo a scheduled inspection by ISI roughly every three years. Schools are given a maximum of two days' notice before inspections, so, like OFSTED inspections, ISI reports tend to offer an accurate and unembellished perspective. In addition to the visit itself, pupils, parents and staff are typically invited to complete confidential questionnaires ahead of the inspection, which feed into the final report.

League tables

The government school performance website allows you to search for league tables in your local area and easily compare options. While league tables are useful indicators of a school's academic performance, they do need to be taken with a pinch of salt. Look out for clear trends over time rather than yearly fluctuations or small percentage differences between schools. Another thing to bear in mind is the intake of a school in rela-tion to the league tables. For example, if children are entering a highly academically selective school and leaving without straight A*/As then this could suggest that they have not made progress. League tables can be useful, but they should only be one part of your decision process.

School website and prospectus

Most schools will offer a prospectus on their website which merits reading, although of course, you must be aware that this is a sales document as much as anything else. As a result of covid-19 restrictions, many more schools now include videos and virtual tours on their websites. It can also be worth following schools you are considering on social media.

If you do not find all the information you are looking for on the school website or in the prospectus, it is well worth ringing up to discover more. In addition, speaking to someone who works at the school will give you some sense of its atmosphere and the kind of people your child will be spending their time with.

Online forums

Online forums, such as Mumsnet, can give you a good insider perspective into schools and a chance to hear unfiltered experiences from parents whose children attend them. However, it is important to remember that everyone posting – whether they are singing a school's praises or tearing them down – will have had a unique experience with the school and may well have their own agenda. Be wary of parents preaching about the school their darling child has just got into, for instance!

Word of mouth

In a similar vein, word of mouth can be a great way to gather more information about a school. Of course, each child's experience will be individual, but if there is consensus around certain advantages or disadvantages then these will soon become apparent. If you can, the best source of information will be a parent whose child is at or has recently left the school, or their child themselves. Do bear in mind, however, that a child who is particularly sporty may not be aware of the school's drama opportunities, for example. Likewise, if the child is the type to constantly push the school's boundaries and your child is not, then their experience will naturally be different.

Once you have whittled down your options to a few promising schools, it is time to get your child involved with the selection process. Take them on open days and be sure to ask them about their thoughts. Ultimately, they are the ones who may have to spend the next seven years at the school in question, so their voice needs to be heard in the decision-making process. They may have some contrary views to you, but if they are particularly adamant about not liking certain schools, they are probably not the best fit. Do also bear in mind, however, that your child's opinions are likely to be influenced by what their friends at school are saying (which in turn will be influenced by their friends' parents).

Open days

Having further narrowed down your list of schools, the best thing to do is to start visiting your options. There is no substitute for getting your feet on the ground and doing some thorough poking around. Open days are a great opportunity to see the facilities on offer, ask questions, speak with staff and pupils, and get a good feel for the school. But remember – open days are a marketing tool, so do not fall for everything you hear!

Most open days have student-led tours or at least offer the chance to speak to current students. Make sure you take this opportunity to ask them about their experiences, as children will be a lot more honest than the school – who, you must remember, are ultimately trying to sell themselves to you. If the school does not let prospective parents speak to pupils, that is a bad sign.

You should also try to speak to teachers. While the Head's speeches will be lovely to hear, they will all likely give similar assurances about high standards, great pastoral care and superb results. Furthermore, your child is unlikely to have much interaction with the Head, whereas they will spend plenty of time with the other teachers. Be on the lookout for engaged, enthusiastic, professional and knowledgeable teachers, and also think about the relationship between the children showing you around the school and the staff – does it seem positive? Likewise, look at how the teachers interact with your child. They should be talking to and engaging with them, not just the parents.

I recommend visiting each of your target schools in person at least once before the formal examination process begins. In my experience, children who attend open events are often better prepared in exams and interviews than those who do not, as they are already familiar with the setting and not as intimidated as they might be on entering a completely new place.

Top questions to ask at open days

What is the school ethos?

This question will give you a sense of the core values of the school. While this is usually information you can find on the school website, it is a good question to ask in person as the reply is likely to be more revealing. You might want to ask members of staff as you are touring, for instance, as their answer will give you a sense of how firmly the ethos is established throughout the school.

What do you like/dislike about the school?

You should get a chance to speak to some of the teachers one-on-one during an open day. If you do, asking for their opinion on the school will give you a fresh and valuable perspective on its merits. A teacher will be able to tell you exactly what they think is special about the school, and potentially offer some context in terms of their experience at previous schools.

If you have the chance, for instance during a student-led tour, this is also a great question to ask current pupils. Other questions you might wish to ask students include:

- What is your favourite/least favourite thing about the school?

- What do you think of the teachers?

- What is your favourite part of a week?

- How much support do you receive, both academic and pastoral?

- What are the extra-curricular activities like?

How do you select staff?

This question will provide a good insight into the standards the school applies to their staff, and how, or if, they keep to that standard throughout their time there.

Other questions about the staff include:

- How often do you hire new staff?

- How long do staff usually stay with you?

- Why do teachers generally leave?

- Where do they go?

How do you help students choose their GCSE and A Level/IB subjects?

The formal exams your child sits during their time at secondary school will affect both their university applications and their career prospects. Making the right choice of subjects is therefore vital, and you want to be sure that your target schools take this decision seriously.

For GCSEs, you may want to ask:

- How many subjects do most children take?

- Is there a maximum and minimum number of subjects they must choose?

- Are there any restrictions around choice (eg that every child must take at least one language or one humanities subject)?

After GCSE, children may take exams for a variety of different qualifications. These include A Level, Pre-U, the IB, and vocational qualifications such as BTECs. Your first question for the school in the area should therefore be: Which examinations do your students sit, and why?

Choosing the right subjects is important, as not only does it affect their university and career options, but spending two years studying a subject they dislike will put a significant strain on your child and should be avoided at all costs.

Questions you may wish to ask the school include:

- Does the school offer any taster sessions for subjects, particularly ones that might not have been an option at GCSE, such as Politics, Economics or Psychology?
- Are there limitations on their choices, such as minimum GCSE grade requirements?
- Does the school restrict certain combinations of subjects, or are students free to choose any combination they wish?

Where do Year 11 and Year 13 leavers go?

It may seem early to consider these questions, but they are crucial. Regardless of whether you have an idea of where your child might want to go to university (if at all), it is important to know how well the secondary school manages their leavers. Most secondary schools should have their Year 13 leavers' university destinations published on their website, but open days allow you to dig a little deeper.

For Year 11 leavers, you may want to ask:

- How many students usually leave after Year 11?
- Why do they opt to leave?
- Where do they usually move on to?
- How many new students do you take on in sixth form?

In terms of Year 13 leavers, it is worth asking how many students do not go on to study at university, whether they take on apprenticeships, and what support is offered for students thinking of taking alternative approaches to higher education. Other questions you may wish to ask include:

- When do you begin preparation for university admissions?

- How much support do you offer when writing personal statements?

- Do you offer additional support for students making Oxbridge or international applications?

- What are some of the popular career paths for alumni?

Higher education preparation is a vital part of any secondary school education, and these questions should help inform you of a school's process.

What do you offer in terms of pastoral care?

Pastoral care is hugely important for children, especially when they are entering their teenage years and facing the stress of formal examinations. Various issues can crop up during secondary school, from peer pressure to mental health issues. It is therefore key that you find out what measures the school takes to care for students beyond academics. You should expect a detailed answer to this question, but also try to ask some specific questions. For example:

- What do you do to combat stress in the run-up to examinations?

- How do you respond to friendship issues between students?

- How do you support children suffering with mental health issues?

- When would you involve parents in a pastoral matter?

Your own gut impressions are vital here too – do you feel that the staff you are speaking to are the sort of people you would feel comfortable going to for support?

How do you handle discipline?

Children will inevitably push boundaries as they grow older and begin to gain more independence. Knowing how a secondary school handles discipline should therefore be an important aspect of your decision. This question will also tell you about the general culture of the school, and from there you can decide whether it is suited to your child and your values as parents.

You may wish to ask for specific examples, such as how they handle minor issues as well as more serious or ongoing problems.

How do you deal with bullying?

Bullying is a serious issue and it can have profound consequences on a child's life. As a parent, you need to affirm that matters of bullying are taken seriously and handled effectively and as soon as possible. You might want to ask:

- How do you handle bullying?

- When would you involve the parents in matters of bullying?

- How do you spot bullying, and what measures are in place to prevent it?

It is also useful to ask questions regarding use of phones and social media, as unfortunately, bullying now frequently takes place online. These questions might include:

- What is your social media/acceptable use of IT policy?

- How do you manage the use of phones throughout the school day?

How many children have left in the last year and why?

During open days, staff are trying to sell the school, so it can be difficult to get a sense of any issues the school might have. Of course, children leave schools for perfectly innocuous reasons all the time, but this type of question may help you cut through some of the sugar-coating and gain a sense of any weak points the school might have.

How diverse is the school?

It is a good idea to get a sense of what demographic of children – and parents – attend a school. A question about diversity will help gauge not only the school's approach to children from different backgrounds, but also around how they teach inclusion and respect.

Specific questions to ask could include:

- How many bursaries do you give out each year?
- How many students are on 100% bursaries?
- How many languages does the student body speak?
- What areas do your students travel in from?

What do you offer to children with SEN or gifted children?

If your child currently has special educational needs, it is vital to find out what support the school can offer. Even if your child does not currently need any additional support, knowing what kind of provision is available is important.

In the next chapter we take a more detailed look at how to apply for schools and the application form itself.

FOUR

The Application Process

I recommend applying to no more than four or five secondary schools. Given that each school will have an individual admissions process, involving interviews, written examinations, and so on, it is simply too much pressure on children to apply for more than this.

It is good practice to include within your list of target schools an aspirational school, an attainable school and a safety school. It can be difficult to assess which schools might fit into these categories for your child, as it is very much case-by-case and what is aspirational for one child might not be for another. It is worth speaking to your child's current school for advice or reaching out to a tuition agency who will have lots of experience with the admissions process for different schools.

It is important that both you and your child are happy with every school on the list and that you do not see some of them, particularly the safety school, as just a 'backup'. One good way to test your feelings about a school is to imagine how you would feel if your child only received one offer for that option. If you would not be delighted about them joining, then do not apply.

The admissions timeline

While I can offer general information about the timeline of the 11 Plus admissions cycle, it is essential to remember that every school is different, and you must check the specific timings and dates at each school your child is applying to.

The first thing to make note of is the application window and deadline for each of your target schools. It is always better to apply earlier rather than later to avoid a last-minute rush. In addition, some schools have a cap for applications and operate on a first-come, first-served basis. Make sure you check if this is the case at any of your target schools and note down when your child needs to apply.

The general timeline looks something like the below.

Summer term of Year 4	Open days and events
April–August of Year 5	Applications open
Mid-October–November of Year 6	Applications close
November of Year 6	Pre-tests
October–December of Year 6	Early interviews (some schools choose to interview before the written examination)
November–January of Year 6	Written examinations (note that some schools will invite children in for the whole day and combine the exam, interview and group activities)
Mid-January–February of Year 6	Post-exam interviews and activity days
February–March of Year 6	Results announced
March of Year 6	Acceptance deadline

How to complete the application form

Independent and grammar schools require parents to fill out an individual application form. These can differ considerably between schools. Many schools moved to online application forms during the pandemic and will likely continue to use these.

Bear in mind:

- Application forms are often only open for short periods of time. Double-check this with the registrars of your target schools and make note of the dates.

- It is not uncommon for families to miss out on a school because they make an error with the school year they are applying for, which is naturally very frustrating. Make sure you get the right one.

- Completing the forms in a last-minute rush can lead to errors. Give yourself plenty of time as they can take longer than expected.

- Good spelling, punctuation, and grammar make a good impression. Take care with your writing when filling out the forms.

- Some schools may ask you to include additional documentation, for example a copy of your child's last school report, some ID documents and a photograph.

What questions will I have to answer?

Potential questions on the application form could include:

- What interests does your child have outside of school?

- What is your child's current academic attainment level?

- How will your child contribute to school life?

- Does your child have any talents or gifts?

- Does your child have any special educational needs?

The following questions can be a bit trickier to answer:

- Which other schools have you applied for?

  This question helps schools to gauge how likely you are to take a place if offered. It also helps them to know which schools they are in competition with. Answering honestly can work in your favour, but it is unwise to write such a long list that it seems you are not really committed to their school and taking more of a scattergun approach.

- Has your child received tutoring to prepare for this entrance exam?

  If your child goes to a state primary school, it is perfectly acceptable to say they have had some tuition to prepare them for elements of the exam not taught in school, such as Verbal and

Non-verbal Reasoning. However, many parents leave this one blank.

What role does a reference play?

Every independent school that you apply for will ask for a detailed reference from your child's primary school (grammar schools do not usually ask for a reference). These can be requested at any time between the application submission and the exam date. The reference plays a large part in the decision-making process for some schools, so you will want to ensure it is as good as possible and a true reflection of your child's talents and potential.

In truth, there is no magic bullet here, and the best approach is to foster a positive and collaborative relationship with the senior leadership of your child's primary school during their time there. This relationship will be different depending on whether your child is at a state school or an independent prep school. Most state schools will happily write the references, but this will never be core to their activities, as it is in a prep school. This is because prep schools are judged by prospective parents on the number of children who win places at popular secondary schools. They are therefore more motivated to write references, although these should still be honest reflections of their opinion of your child. Prep schools are used to writing references and are likely to have a detailed file about your child with notes about their achievements and positive accomplishments ready to go. It can also be useful to have a meeting with the senior leadership team to let them know about any particular accomplishments your child might have outside of school, such as attending a youth orchestra.

Some secondary schools simply ask for your child's most recent school report. If this is their policy then make sure you include plenty about your child's achievements, hobbies and interests on the application form. Also make sure your child is well prepped for the interview so they can re-emphasise these qualities at this stage.

A word of warning – many schools will ask about a child's family in the reference. It may count against you if you have been unnecessarily demanding, unpleasant or aggressive in your dealings with the school. Ultimately, you and the school are working towards the same goal: to ensure your child transfers with ease to a secondary school where they will flourish. Be nice.

PART TWO
TAKING THE 11 PLUS EXAMINATION

Part two of *How to Pass the 11 Plus* focusses on the assessment process itself, including the subjects examined, exam technique and interviews. For your child to succeed in the 11 Plus, you need a clear game plan and focused preparation. In this part, in Chapter 7, I set out a year-long programme which will ensure your child is fully prepared in good time for every part of the assessment process, so there is no risk of a last-minute rush.

We'll begin by going into each element of the written exam in more detail so you can better understand what your child will be tested on and how you can help them prepare. Then I set out the twelve-month programme.

To succeed in the 11 Plus, you need to factor in more than just syllabus acquisition. By the time the exams roll around, good exam technique should be second nature to your child. Children will also have a much better chance at passing the 11 Plus if they have sat several mock exams under exam conditions. It is also important to factor daily reading into your preparation as this will put your child at a big advantage. I'll go into detail on each of these additional factors, as well as provide tips on how to help your child enjoy the learning process.

FIVE

Exam Subjects In Detail

In this chapter, we'll look at each academic subject tested and how best to prepare for the individual papers that make up the 11 Plus examination. Each subject is of equal importance, and it is better to reach for a good level in all of them rather than brilliance in one at the expense of the others. Parents with children in state school primaries should be particularly careful to ensure enough effort is given to developing Verbal and Non-verbal Reasoning skills, which are not part of the National Curriculum and hence will not be taught in their school.

English

The 11 Plus English exam will cover the entire Year 6 syllabus. You can download the full syllabus from the government website,[4] but its key components include:

- Correct use of spelling, punctuation and grammar.

- Vocabulary, including using (but not overusing) similes, metaphors and personification for effect.

- Consistent, legible handwriting – ideally cursive.

- Creative writing: Children must be able to develop imaginative detail, develop and shape use of language and ideas to suit the genre and adopt and maintain a clear viewpoint throughout.

- Understanding of genre: Children must have a good grasp of the features of different text types and be able to use these confidently and sometimes blend or adapt them, while making a deliberate attempt to maintain a reader's interest.

- Organisation of writing: Children must write in paragraphs made up of appropriate strings of sentences and make decisions about how to effectively structure the whole text. Appropriate

---

4   Department for Education, 'National curriculum in England: English programmes of study' (Department for Education, 2014) https://tinyurl.com/yc74zacn, accessed 23 December 2021

use of adverbs and connectives to link paragraphs will also impress.

- Grouping ideas and linking them together: Children must consistently structure texts using cohesive paragraphs confidently and precisely. The use of tense, person and connective must also be consistent and appropriate throughout.

Structure of the English exam

Most schools divide the English exam into two sections – comprehension and creative writing.

Comprehension

Students will be asked to read a short prose passage and then answer comprehension questions. The comprehension questions will test understanding of the passage, in terms of both the content and the writer's use of language.

To succeed, students need to be able to:

- Read passages and texts from a variety of sources carefully. Demonstrate the ability to identify and extract information.

- Explain the purpose of a text.

- Demonstrate the ability to summarise sections of writing and identify the main point.

- Support answers using quotations from the text.

- Explain the meaning of words within the text and understand their usage within the context of the passage.

- Demonstrate an awareness of how word choice, vocabulary, grammar and punctuation affect the meaning of a text.

- Recognise literary devices, explain how they create certain effects on the reader, and explain the writer's purpose when using such words.[5]

Creative writing

Candidates will be asked to write a description or section of narrative, usually in response to a written or visual stimulus. The key criteria are clarity, fluency, accuracy of written expression, imaginative flair and good presentation.

Candidates need to demonstrate an ability to:

- Write using clearly structured paragraphs.

- Organise ideas effectively.

- Convey feelings and opinions in an accurate way.

- Write imaginatively and descriptively.

---

5   The Tutoress, *11+ English Syllabus* (The Tutoress, 2020) www
     .thetutoress.com/s/11-English-Syllabus-TheTutoresscom-1.pdf,
     accessed 23 December 2021

- Use a range of literary devices in their compositions.

- Respond accurately to the title, question or stimulus given.

- Use stimuli as the basis for producing an effective story.

Preparing for success in 11 Plus English

Comprehension

Children who read every day in the run-up to the exam will have a distinct advantage over those who do not in both the comprehension and creative writing sections. For comprehension, I recommend exposing your child to some classic texts, as these are disproportionally represented in 11 Plus comprehensions because of their difficult vocabulary and syntax. It may throw your child unnecessarily if they have never been exposed to this kind of language and grammar. Good examples of these are *Little Women*, *Treasure Island* or *Oliver Twist*. Read the whole story with them and ask them questions as you go along. Some questions you might ask include:

- What do you think the character is thinking or feeling?

- What does this passage make you feel? How has the writer achieved this?

- What do you think will happen next?

If they are struggling with a particular word, rather than telling them what it means immediately, ask them to try and figure it out from the context. It is good to try and build up new vocabulary whenever you can.

Creative writing

Topics set for 11 Plus creative writing pieces tend to have the same common themes. For this reason, it can be useful for your child to build a mental library of 'stock' stories that they can draw on in the exam. Children do need to be flexible however, and a student is likely to be marked down if the marker feels they are simply regurgitating a memorised piece of writing (especially if it does not fit with the title). However, having a few ideas already in their mind will give students a good starting point and will help them write something in the allocated time that demonstrates their skills. Set aside some time each week for your child to practise writing in different genres.

These are some of the themes that frequently come up:

- Being lost, scared or alone
- Doing something exciting or achieving something ('The best day of my life was...')
- Having an adventure
- Being in a city or in the countryside

Here are some examples of stimuli for story writing from previous 11 Plus past papers:

- A lost key
- A farewell party
- An attempted robbery
- A surprising spy

Other formats for the creative writing section can be opening sentences, such as:

- It was a while before I realised my cat could talk…
- I do not know what that noise was…

Or they can be titles:

- Moving Houses
- The New Pupils
- The Storm

Students might also be asked to write:

- A diary entry
- A letter to persuade
- An article to inform, discuss or instruct
- A book review

In terms of practising story writing, some excellent resources include the *Descriptosaurus* books[6] and Mrs Wordsmith resources, including books, games and worksheets.[7] I also recommend the RSL Education 11 Plus comprehension books as they have detailed specimen answers with mark allocations.[8]

In addition to regularly practising their imaginative writing skills, it cannot be said enough that the best preparation your child can do for the creative writing exam is regular reading. This will help them to gain a breadth of vocabulary, understand the structure of a good story and help them to think imaginatively.

Reading to help pass

A daily reading habit can be the difference between success and failure in the 11 Plus process. Although most parents understand the importance of reading for their child's progress and development, few appreciate its specific relevance and importance to exam preparation.

For context, here are some of the most common reasons that children struggle in their 11 Plus examinations:

- Insufficient breadth of vocabulary
- Slow reading skills

---

6   www.descriptosaurus.org
7   www.mrswordsmith.com
8   www.rsleducational.co.uk

- Poor punctuation, grammar and spelling skills

- Failing to read exam questions properly

- Struggling with concentration and stamina

Reading can boost performance in all these areas. A child who reads every day will have a wider vocabulary; better spelling, grammar and punctuation skills; and stronger concentration than a child who does not read or who reads only occasionally. These are skills that are best built up gradually over time rather than crammed for in a few weeks. A daily reading habit is therefore, in our opinion, the best way to develop them.

Below we go into more detail on the areas that daily reading will improve for children taking the 11 Plus, which will benefit their performance not only in the English exam but in the other subject exams too.

Word meanings: Word definitions are often included in Verbal Reasoning exams and are vital for the comprehension paper. While even avid readers may not be able to precisely define every word they read, they will have built up a good understanding of how to gauge meaning based on context.

Spelling: The more frequently children read, the more likely they are to notice when a word is spelled incorrectly or when there are mistakes in grammar or punctuation.

Speed and fluency: Regular readers will usually read more rapidly and fluently than those who do not read often. For comprehension exercises, it is essential to be able to read quickly while still being aware of meaning.

Concentration: Reading every day helps to develop concentration. Many exams can last for an hour or more, so being able to focus consistently throughout means your child will make fewer mistakes.

Creative writing: Reading stories regularly means your child will develop an understanding of what it is that makes a story engaging and enthralling. They will also understand how a story is structured and how that affects the reader's experience. Regular readers are also more likely to read a variety of types of story, which will help them to come up with story ideas in the exam.

Relieving stress: Reading regularly is a pleasure in itself, so rather than adding to the pressure your child may feel about exams, it is actually something that will help them to relax. The underlying benefits it provides for learning will happen without them even realising.

When should children start reading to prepare for their entrance exam?

Regardless of exams, reading is something that children should be doing every day. Reading has a lifelong positive impact on a child, affecting not only their education but their health, wellbeing and creativity. Most children have become independent readers by Year 3, and from then on they should ideally read every day, even when other schoolwork starts to become more demanding in Year 5. Remember, if a child continues to read every day throughout the whole of the lead-up to the 11 Plus, it will be extremely useful for the exam, but it will also be a way of relieving the pressure they may be feeling.

What books should children read to prepare for their entrance exam?

The secret to success in helping your child get into the habit of reading every day is to start with stories they love. Variety can come later: the important thing is that reading should be something they're excited about. Children also like repetition, so series of books such as *Harry Potter, Pippi Longstocking*, or *Flat Stanley* are great places to start. It can also help if their friends can recommend books that they have enjoyed. As always, spend some time reading along with your child as well as giving them time to read alone. Even children who are confident solo readers need to be heard reading aloud so that their accuracy can be monitored and their understanding of what they are reading can be checked through questioning and discussion. See our resources section for more ideas of books your child might enjoy reading.

Classic books

Sometimes a classic book may come up in an 11 Plus comprehension. As we have discussed above, classic books often use more difficult vocabulary and syntax than modern books, and it can come as a shock if an exam situation is the first time your child has experienced this. It's important to make sure your child has been exposed to some classic fiction, especially if you are applying to an academic or competitive school. Not only will it improve your child's vocabulary, comprehension and writing skills, but it will help them to understand literary techniques such as alliteration, similes and metaphors, and why these are used. They will also develop their skills in using the context to work out what new or difficult words might mean.

Children can sometimes find classic books difficult to read, but even if you read some to your child yourself, they will still derive the benefits. You know better than anyone what types of stories your child likes best, but you might want to try *Black Beauty*, *The Sword in the Stone*, or *The Secret Garden*. Otherwise, plenty of recommendations can be found online or in your local bookshop.

What if my child does not enjoy fiction?

If your child doesn't enjoy reading fiction, there is no need to despair as there are plenty of other things they can read to develop their skills. Magazines are a great option, for instance. Some of our favourite children's magazines include:

- *The Week Junior*

- *Aquila*

- *The Caterpillar*

- *Scoop*

- *Anorak*

- *Kookie*

- *The Loop*

- *National Geographic Kids*

Picture books, graphic novels, illustrated fiction, diary-style books and audiobooks can also bring stories to life in an appealing way for reluctant readers.

School-specific preparation

As always, it is important to understand the type of English exam your target school sets. Most schools will stick to a repeated formula in respect of comprehension styles and story prompts. Some schools will always select a classic text for their comprehension, knowing the difficult vocabulary and syntax will challenge applicants. Alternatively, some schools often use a non-fiction text such as a newspaper article, again providing vocabulary challenges for children who are used to fiction only.

Many schools have past papers on their websites. Download these and look at the style of questions, the types of text selected for comprehensions and the kind of story stimuli used. Doing your research as a parent will pay dividends and allow you to be a lot more focussed in your preparation.

Maths

The 11 Plus Maths exam will cover the entire Year 6 syllabus. You can download the full syllabus from the government website,[9] but its key components include:

- Using numbers and placing value accurately

- Addition, subtraction, multiplication and division

- Fractions, including decimals and percentages

- Ratio and proportion

- Basic algebra

- Measurement

- Geometry

- Handling data and statistics

---

9 Department for Education, 'National curriculum in England: Mathematics programmes of study' (Department for Education, 2021) https://tinyurl.com/236p6k7n, accessed 23 December 2021government website

Structure of the Maths exam

The Maths examination is usually one paper lasting between 45 minutes and an hour. The exam tends to start with short questions testing basic mental maths, which your child will need to move through with speed. These early questions are quite easy and students should be able to answer them confidently and quickly before moving on to the more complex, problem-based questions that follow. Exam technique is critical as students need to ensure they leave enough time to answer the harder questions later in the paper.

The final quarter of the Maths paper usually tests children with questions they won't have seen before. This is where children can really differentiate themselves. It is vital that pupils get to this stage of the paper in time to properly attempt some of these questions, especially if they are applying for a scholarship place.

Preparing for success in 11 Plus Maths

As with every aspect of the 11 Plus, speed is of the utmost importance in the Maths exam. The key to achieving this is a secure knowledge and quick recall of times tables and number bonds. Your child should focus on these in Years 4 and 5 at school and continue to practise them throughout their 11 Plus preparation year, no matter how good they are at Maths. There are several excellent apps that gamify the acquisition and practice of these skills so that children enjoy their learning. These include:

- Hit the Button
- King of Maths
- Squeebles Times Tables
- Times Tables Rock Stars

These are all simple and effective ways of practising quick-fire recall and other mental arithmetic skills.

Remember that mathematical ability will also play a large role in your child's Non-verbal Reasoning score. It may be tested in your child's interview, with mental maths and logic questions, so maths skills are essential to success in the 11 Plus.

Reasoning

The Reasoning exam is split into two sections: Verbal Reasoning and Non-verbal Reasoning.

Reasoning is intended by schools to be a pure test of ability and skill rather than learned knowledge. As such, some parents assume that it cannot be prepared for, but this is not the case. Although your child will start out with a certain ability level in reasoning, there are a finite number of types of Verbal and Non-verbal Reasoning questions, and it is easy to practise and improve on them all if you start early and work systematically. See below for our breakdown of each type of reasoning exam and our tips on how you can further help your child improve their score.

Practise Verbal and Non-verbal Reasoning every day, beginning in the summer holidays of Year 5. Little and often usually works best – the Bond or CGP ten-minute test books are perfect for this.

Not every school will include reasoning as part of their written examination, so it is vital to check this before beginning your preparations. Similarly, reasoning is the part of the assessment that varies most strongly between the two boards (GL and CEM), so again it is essential to identify which type of test your child will be sitting. Few schools will put past Reasoning papers on their website, so if you know whether they are using GL or CEM you can purchase the relevant resources to help them practise.

Finally, make sure you know what kind of reasoning assessment your child will be sitting (eg digital, written, multiple-choice, etc). Some digital tests do not allow children to go back at the end to check their work or answer difficult questions, whereas this would be standard practice in a written paper.

Verbal Reasoning

Verbal Reasoning tests a child's ability to understand and logically work through concepts and problems expressed in words. The tests tell schools how well a child can extract and work with meanings, information and implications from text. It assesses critical thinking skills and the ability to apply knowledge to solve word problems.

Parents are sometimes surprised that Verbal Reasoning assessments also include cracking number codes and completing number sequences. There can be some challenging maths on the Verbal Reasoning papers, including square numbers and algebra, so your child must be prepared for this too.

These are some of the most common types of Verbal Reasoning questions. It is important that your child knows how to approach these and has practised them sufficiently.

Sequences:

- Numerical sequences, including square, cube and prime numbers
- Letter sequences
- Letter connections
- Alphabet analogies

Code-breaking:

- Word-number codes
- Word-letter codes

Making up words:

- Using rules to make up words
- Word ladders

Logic puzzles:

- Fact puzzles
- Logic puzzles

Word meanings and vocabulary-based questions:

- Synonyms
- Antonyms
- Homonyms
- Homophones
- Homographs
- Definitions
- Word categories

Preparing for success in 11 Plus Verbal Reasoning

By far the best long-term preparation for Verbal Reasoning success is to create a daily reading habit with your child. There is an urban myth which states that children who pass the 11 Plus know 10,000 more words than children who do not pass. While this should be taken with a pinch of salt, there is an underlying truth to this statement. Vocabulary acquisition takes a long time to develop and is essential for success. It should not, therefore, be crammed last-minute.

In addition to maintaining a daily reading habit, you can help your child to succeed in the 11 Plus by:

- Playing word-based board games such as 'Scrabble', 'Bananagrams' and 'Boggle' with your child.

- Playing hangman, crosswords, word searches and Tetris with your child.

- Practising spelling and grammar with tests, eg asking your child the difference between 'there', 'they're' and 'their'.

Although speed is vital in the Verbal Reasoning exam, it is important that children read the questions carefully. Encourage your child to take their Verbal Reasoning practice slowly at first as they learn how to approach the questions, and to concentrate on speed only when their knowledge is secure.

Non-verbal Reasoning

Non-verbal Reasoning tests students' ability to understand and logically work through concepts and problems expressed pictorially or diagrammatically. Schools want to see how well a child can extract meaning, information, and implications from pictures, without the support of their textual or linguistic skills.

As with Verbal Reasoning, each child will have a natural affinity for this topic but can certainly improve and should practise all iterations of the test.

Common types of Non-verbal Reasoning questions include:

- Working out what a shape would look like when folded or unfolded

- Identifying the mirror image of a shape

- Figuring out the next shape in a sequence

- Figuring out the odd one out in a sequence

- Finding identical shapes in a group of shapes

- Identifying what shapes look like when rotated

- Codes

I highly recommend checking the websites of your target schools for more information on what questions are usually asked.

Spatial reasoning

There is currently a clear trend for spatial reasoning in Non-verbal Reasoning papers. Spatial reasoning concerns the ability to picture shapes in 3D and to mentally move them around. Typical questions might ask how an image has been reflected, rotated or translated as part of a sequence, or involve constructing 3D shapes. Some schools include these questions in their assessments because they believe they identify children who will excel in Maths and STEM subjects. Parents need not worry, though, as with all aspects of reasoning there are only so many potential questions and these can all be practised thoroughly.

Preparing for success in 11 Plus Non-verbal Reasoning

First, aim to familiarise your child with each type of Non-verbal Reasoning question that they might come across. Once children are familiar, aim for accuracy. It is important for children to work methodically in Non-verbal Reasoning papers, focussing on one aspect at a time, and to identify the correct answer by first eliminating wrong answers. Children who try to solve Non-verbal Reasoning questions by looking for the right answer are often caught out due to the complexity of the figures they are working with. As with all exams, it does not matter how bright your child is if they do not read the instructions carefully.

From September of Year 6, you must encourage your child to work through their Non-verbal Reasoning practice at speed. They will need to pick up one mark per minute, while maintaining accuracy. This is an essential element of their preparation as reasoning tests are notoriously time-pressured. There is no point in your child answering accurately but only getting halfway through the paper in the allotted time, yet this is a common hurdle to success.

Beyond formal practice questions, all the following will develop your child's understanding of 3D shapes and number patterns:

- Building with Lego, completing jigsaw puzzles or trying to solve a Rubik's cube are all excellent ways to develop spatial awareness.

- Sudokus, riddles and word puzzles can all enhance problem-solving abilities and lateral-thinking skills.

- Strategic games such as chess and draughts are brilliant for decision-making and thinking ahead.

Remember, promoting a positive and playful approach to revision will help achieve stress-free success.

SIX
Exam Technique

No matter how bright your child is and how hard they have studied, they will struggle to pass their 11 Plus exams successfully without honing their exam technique.

This can be a challenge because the concepts of good exam technique can be difficult for children to understand. In our opinion, the best way to help your child with exam technique is to provide them with plenty of opportunity to practise in realistic situations. This is why mock exams are a vital part of our twelve-month programme.

Good exam technique is something that should be developed over a long period of time. Small, regular assessments should be built into your 11 Plus preparation programme and these will assist in developing good exam technique. As you will see in the twelve-month programme, I recommend beginning mock exam papers during the Summer term of Year 5 and summer holidays and to focus more exclusively on improving exam technique and speed towards the end of the summer holidays and into the first term of Year 6. Ideally, students should be confident in their subject knowledge before beginning to tackle exam technique.

As always with the 11 Plus exams, it is vital to find out the type of test your child will be taking, as different formats require different types of exam technique.

Questions you might consider asking your target schools include:

- Will they be sitting the ISEB Pre-Test?

- Will they be answering multiple-choice questions?

- Will they be answering long-form written questions?

- Will they be sitting digital or paper-based tests, or both?

Each type of test requires different exam techniques, but they do all have one thing in common: time pressure.

Timing

The importance of timing in the 11 Plus exams cannot be stressed enough. No matter how talented and well-prepared your child is, if they do not answer enough questions in their exam, they will not pick up enough marks to do well. This is one of the most common hurdles to success in the 11 Plus assessments.

This problem is usually particularly acute in children who attend state primary schools, as they are less likely to have been regularly tested in school under exam conditions and time pressure. Yet all children and parents need to be cognisant of the importance of timing and prepare accordingly.

First, ensure your child knows how their exam will be timed. Timing can differ across exam boards (eg CEM or GL), regions and individual schools, so – as always – check the admissions sections of the websites of the schools you are interested in. Some entrance exams consist of individually timed sections, for instance, while others allow between 45 and 75 minutes to complete the whole paper. Your child will have a good view of a clock during their examination and they should be reminded of the importance of checking the time frequently. They might also wish to wear a watch for this reason. It is important that they understand how long to spend on each question – there is no point agonising over a question that is only worth two marks and then rushing through one worth ten.

Approaching difficult questions

There will always be some questions in your child's exam that they find harder than others. Remind your child not to panic if this happens. Every student has different topics or styles of question that they find easier and others that they find more difficult. What is important is for your child to recognise when a question is slowing them down too much. Rather than wasting time trying to figure out a single answer, it is usually better to move on and use the time to complete other questions that they find easier. Some children find it useful to put a small mark or star next to any questions they have missed, as this helps them to easily find it and have another go at it later if they have time.

In the case of multiple-choice papers, I do not recommend skipping questions. Instead, encourage your child to narrow down the options as much as possible and then to make an informed estimate. They will still have a good chance of getting it right and it prevents the issue of putting the next answer in the wrong place.

No matter how much preparation they do, your child should be prepared to face a question or a style of question that they have not encountered before. Again, remind them not to panic. Their hard work preparing for the exam will have given them the skills required to tackle the unexpected with confidence.

Checking over work

Given the tight timings of the exam, many students do not get round to checking their work at all. This means your child will be at a significant advantage if they do have some checking time, and they should use it wisely.

It is easy to make small mistakes under pressure, so even if your child is sure they have completed everything correctly they should spend any spare time they have checking over their workings and their answers.

In Maths papers, students should check for small mistakes in operations, for instance, by redoing sums. In English written answers, they should check for spelling and grammar mistakes. In all papers, students should ensure they have read the question properly and answered with a sufficient level of detail.

Types of exam

Multiple-choice

Many 11 Plus exams use a multiple-choice format. This means that the paper is likely to be marked by computer, so it is crucial that your child fills out the answer sheet correctly and clearly. To avoid marking errors, your child must:

- Draw a straight and complete line through the answer box so that the computer reads the correct answer.

- Rub out wrong answers sufficiently so that the optical eye of the computer does not read them.

- Make sure the answers match up with the correct question in the question paper. For instance, if your child leaves a question out, they must not forget this on the answer sheet because every answer afterwards would be in the wrong place and hence marked incorrect.

Digital exams

Digital exams, such as the ISEB Pre-Test, demand specific exam techniques because of their unique format. All questions are compulsory and candidates cannot move forward until an answer has been chosen from four multiple-choice options. Students need to be comfortable making educated guesses by eliminating obviously wrong answers and then trying to work out which is most likely from the remaining options. They must also understand the time constraints of the test, and not waste too much time prevaricating over the options.

Students also need to understand that they cannot go backwards in digital tests. This means they cannot leave difficult questions until the end, which they may be used to doing in written papers. Instead, they must practise learning to deal with each question as it comes up.

Remember that most digital tests are adaptive, meaning the questions get easier or more difficult depending on the performance of the candidate. This is why accuracy is so important in the early, 'easier' stages of the test, where children may make silly mistakes. Even if your child is capable of tackling harder questions, if they trip up early on then they will not get the chance to answer these. This could prevent them from demonstrating their full potential.

Candidates should get plenty of practice completing online tests under exam conditions so that they can get a feel for the format. This will help students to get used to working under time pressure, reading the questions thoroughly and managing their time efficiently. ISEB have a familiarisation test which students can practise taking, and you can also obtain practice tests using sites like Atom Learning.

Staying calm

It is normal for students to be nervous before an exam, but it is important for your child not to let this feeling overwhelm them and hamper their performance. Simple relaxation strategies such as deep breathing can be an essential tool if your child has a tendency to be nervous.

As a parent, you have a major role to play in not making the exams overly stressful for your child. Remind them regularly that the exam is not the be all and end all, and that you are proud of them simply for doing their best. Learning should be something that children enjoy rather than something they find stressful. There are many ways you can help your child stay calm, focussed and healthy while preparing for the 11 Plus examination, starting with understanding your child's learning style.

Your child's learning style

Every child is different, and every child learns in different ways. Making sure that children learn in a way that suits their specific style can make a huge difference to their progress and, in particular, to their wellbeing. It can be especially powerful when managing the education of a child with additional educational needs.

Is your child a visual, auditory, reading/ writing or kinaesthetic learner?

Visual learners like whatever they are learning to be presented through images such as pictures, diagrams or mind maps. They often like to draw or make notes with little illustrations to help them take in information. Printed handouts or notes can help them to process talks or presentations, as can whiteboards and videos.

Auditory learners learn best by listening, rather than writing notes. They often speak their thoughts aloud or read aloud to themselves to help them process information. Discussing ideas or question-and-answer sessions often help auditory learners, as do talks, videos that include the spoken word, audiobooks or recordings, rather than writing notes.

Reading/writing learners like to learn through the written word, for example by researching, reading articles, books or online information, and writing in diaries or journals. They can sometimes be confused with visual learners, but the key is that reading/writing learners always prefer to use writing to express themselves. They like to learn through writing essays or written projects, and find it helpful to have enough time to work through their ideas on paper.

Kinaesthetic or tactile learners like to learn by doing, and especially by using their hands and bodies. They are often fidgety, so it can be helpful to ask them to move around as they learn, for instance by acting out scenes from a book or walking up and down as they try to learn information. Practical activities such as handling physical objects or working with Lego can also help them to absorb facts or abstract concepts.

If your child has difficulty concentrating on the task at hand, try approaching it differently, ideally according to their preferred learning style. Is there a way to introduce something tactile, auditory, written or visual to the task?

Plan your schedule

The idea that children thrive in structured environments is nothing new, but this practice can extend beyond the school timetable too. By developing an easy-to-understand schedule for your children and providing them with a clear understanding of what is expected from them each day, you will equip them with valuable life skills – timekeeping and communication, for example – as well as hone their ability to make decisions, accept responsibility and develop a good work ethic.

This sort of structure is important at all times of the year, but particularly in the lead-up to exams like the 11 Plus. Marking the calendar with the specific date and planning their activities for the days ahead will reduce their stress and anxiety and make the prospect of sitting an important exam more manageable.

Focus on fun

It can be hard, but try to focus on what your child enjoys rather than what they struggle with. Spend time with them doing the things they love. If they are a bookworm, take them to a library or a bookshop and let them spend hours picking out new things to read. If they are musical, encourage them to take up an instrument – this also happens to be a great brain activity that can improve mathematical and spatial reasoning.

Setting specific intentions can help, too, particularly if your child is keen on competitive sports or challenges: the 'Sport and Literacy' programmes run by the Literacy Trust have proved a huge success, helping thousands of sport-obsessed kids tap into a love of reading by making the act of reading a challenge and setting tangible goals.

Mock exams

Mock exams are a crucial part of a child's preparation for entrance exams. They help to:

- Give children a realistic run-through of the test by replicating exam conditions.

- Improve time management skills and speed.

- Settle nerves and reduce anxiety by allowing children to get used to exam conditions before they sit the real thing.

- Provide a useful gauge of current attainment and indication of areas that require improvement.

When should my child sit mock exams?

In the twelve-month programme, children sit mock exams towards the end of their 11 Plus journey.

The main purpose of a mock exam is to experience realistic exam conditions and practise good exam technique. Although students should be secure in their subject knowledge by this stage, practising confronting questions they are unsure about is also an important part of the mock exam experience.

Read on for an in-depth look at the twelve-month programme.

SEVEN

The Twelve-Month Programme

Our proposed twelve-month preparation programme consists of three main elements:

- **Phase One:** Acquisition of Year 5 and Year 6 syllabus

- **Phase Two:** Extensive question practice

- **Phase Three:** Improving exam technique and speed

Your child will naturally continue to develop their understanding of the syllabus while they are working on exam questions and speed, but this structure will help you to know where their learning should be by certain points in the year.

Ideally, students will complete Phase One by Easter of Year 5, Phase Two by the end of the summer holidays of Year 5 and Phase Three during the summer holidays and into the first term of Year 6. 11 Plus testing can start as early as October of Year 6, so this leaves a bit of extra time at the end of summer.

If your child is already behind on this timetable, do not panic! You might consider setting up tutoring sessions or enrolling them in a holiday course to help bring them up to speed.

Phase One – Acquisition of Year 5 and Year 6 syllabus

One of the most difficult aspects of the 11 Plus is that students need to have learned the whole of the Year 6 Maths and English syllabus by the time they need to sit their exams. Prep schools often gear up for this by teaching the Year 6 syllabus to their cohorts by the end of Year 5, leaving the autumn of Year 6 free to practise papers and work on exam technique. However, this should not be assumed. Parents need to be careful to ensure their child has covered the whole syllabus in time. Children simply cannot score marks on topics they have not been taught.

As mentioned previously, state primaries do not teach children the required Year 6 syllabus early. Parents with children at state schools therefore need to make alternative arrangements for this extra work to ensure it is completed in time.

During this phase, you should begin practising reasoning, too. Again, prep schools often teach reasoning, but state primaries are unlikely to. In both instances parents need to understand the required standard and ensure that their child learns reasoning techniques, masters the key question types and can work through reasoning papers at speed.

Phase Two – Extensive question practice

Once children have been taught all the topics on the syllabus, they need to practise questions extensively to gain familiarity, confidence and speed. For example, they may have understood how to solve fractions when taught as a discrete topic and solved them mathematically, but in entrance exams they will need to unpick wordy questions to work out the underlying fraction problem they need to solve. By practising 11 Plus style questions and working through past exam papers, students will learn how to do this quickly and accurately.

Again, ensure your child is practising with resources that mirror the type of tests their target schools will be using (eg CEM, GL, Atom). I recommend buying the resources that best reflect the exam of your first-choice school.

Past papers

During the Summer term of Year 5, download and print off all the past papers available on your target schools' websites. There will hopefully be at least two per school. It can also be useful to download some past papers from schools of a similar academic standard.

Create a spreadsheet noting all the exam papers you have. Then work backwards from the date of the exams, placing a date for each paper to be completed at regular intervals. Hopefully, this will mean your child completes one or two papers per week over the summer holidays and into the Autumn term.

During this phase, do not worry too much if your child takes longer than the allocated time to complete the past papers. It is more important that they work through all the questions and, once it has been marked, go through it again to do their corrections. It is vital that students understand not just what they got wrong, but why. This will help to focus the work that still needs to be done.

Summer holidays

It is important that your child has time to relax over the summer holidays and be well rested before beginning Year 6. The object of the summer holidays is therefore to maintain momentum. Continue with your past paper schedule and begin practising Verbal and Non-verbal Reasoning every day (remember, ten minutes a day over an extended period is far better than last-minute cramming).

You should also encourage your child to read lots over the holidays. Try to read more challenging books, such as classic texts, with them, so that you can discuss the vocabulary and do some basic comprehension questions. As we have looked at already, a regular reading habit is one of the most important things you can do to support your child's chances in the 11 Plus.

Phase Three – Improving exam technique and speed

At this point, your child should be secure in their subject knowledge, have practised lots of questions and be familiar with the style of typical exam papers. Their exam technique and speed should have developed from practice but this is the point to really nail them down.

As a reminder, the most important elements of good exam technique are:

- Leaving questions that one is struggling with and coming back to them at the end if there is time.

- Giving an answer for every multiple-choice question. If students are unsure, they should try to narrow down the options as much as possible and then make an informed choice. It is not worth leaving any question blank.

- Taking appropriate time on each question relative to the marks available (eg spending longer on a ten-mark question that a one-mark question).

The best way to improve speed is to practise. The more questions your child practises, the more familiar they will be with different formats and how to answer them. Question practice will also help your child with their syllabus recall, so it is a great way for them to revise.

Prep for interviews

In this phase, you will also need to start thinking about preparation for interviews and group assessments, as these usually take place between September and February of Year 6. See our next chapter for more information on the interview and group assessments.

Countdown to the exam

The final week

In the week before your child's exam, it is a good idea to refamiliarise them with the format of the school in question's assessments. For instance, you could look over one of the past papers they have already completed together.

The night before

Do not try and get your child to learn anything the night before an exam. Instead, actively try to help your child relax, ideally with something more fun than zoning out in front of the TV. Whatever game they love to play will work well, such as Uno or Monopoly. Try to let them win! The aim is to get them laughing.

When it is time for bed, make sure to tell them that you are proud of all their hard work and wherever they end up at school will be just right for them. Really try to avoid placing pressure on them at this stage. Getting your child in bed on time is crucial.

From your perspective, make sure you know directions to the school, what the traffic and weather will be like, where you can park and what your child is allowed to take in with them. You want to avoid any surprises on the day. It is a good idea to pack your child's bag the night before to avoid a rush in the morning.

The day of the exam

Make sure your child has a good breakfast and that you leave in plenty of time. You want to ensure they do not pick up on any stress from you, so try to exude calmness and reassurance at all times.

There can be lots of children arriving at the school on exam day, which may be unnerving for your child.

Each school will have its own drop-off procedure, and some will not allow you to stay with your child for long, but if you can, try to give them a nice reassuring hug before they go in.

If you are applying to several schools, your child will likely have several 11 Plus tests to sit. They will probably be most nervous before the first exam, but you should monitor them carefully throughout the duration of their 11 Plus tests to ensure they are not becoming overwhelmed.

It is important for parents to relax and trust that their child's hard work will pay off. While it may be difficult not to let your nerves show, your child needs to feel confident on exam day. If you look anxious, it will likely rub off on them and could knock the confidence you have spent a year building. I have seen parents waving flash cards in front of their children as they walk into the exam room – do not do this. This will only unsettle your child and place pressure on them, which is not what they need before a big exam.

We will go into more detail on your role as a parent and the ways you can support your child's mental, physical and emotional health during the 11 Plus in Chapter 11, 'Supporting Your Child's Wellbeing'.

After the exam

After the exam, make sure you are there on time to pick them up. Avoid asking too much about how it went as they may not wish to discuss it. It can be nice to treat them to their favourite dinner or TV programme in the evening as a well done.

EIGHT

The Interview

Like many elements of the 11 Plus, the specifics of the interview will depend on the schools your child is applying to. Some schools interview all applicants, sometimes on the day of the written exam itself, while others will only interview students who do well in the written examinations. Some schools ask children to perform a group interview and/or activity as an alternative. Some do not interview at all. As always, do your research before you begin preparations, but be aware that most interviews take place between September and February of Year 6.

Regardless of format, the interview is a vital part of the school entrance process. Schools are placing increasing importance on how well children communicate, demonstrate intelligent reasoning, and show evidence of an enquiring mind. The importance of preparation therefore cannot be understated.

You want your child to present themselves naturally and confidently but not to give responses that appear rehearsed. Your child should be prepared to answer questions honestly and intelligently and to show evidence of an enquiring mind. We will discuss how best to prepare children for interviews later in this chapter, but it is important to avoid overpreparation as this can lead to a wooden interview style.

Interview format

Most schools conduct one-on-one interviews on school premises with a teacher or senior member of staff. Usually, interviews are between fifteen and twenty-five minutes long. You should check your target schools' websites to see if they offer any specific guidance of what their interview process entails. Sometimes children are asked to complete a pre-interview form detailing their interests and achievements, and sometimes they are asked to bring an object of interest they would like to talk about with them. At some schools they may even be asked to prepare a short presentation on a topic that interests them.

Digital interviews

Due to the covid-19 pandemic, in 2020 many interviews took place online over Zoom to comply with social distancing regulations. While many schools were eager to return to in-person interviews, others saw an advantage in digital interviews that allowed for faster turnover times and avoided the inevitable disruption that interviews create at schools. They also allow more flexibility for children living abroad.

Digital interviews pose some new challenges to children and require different preparation. Children must learn how to begin, join and end a video call, what to do if various technical problems present and how to make an impact on screen. When setting up for an online interview, make sure it is in a quiet place, with good internet connection, where your child is comfortable. It can be a good idea to practise using the platform in a low-pressure context, such as calling their friends, so they are familiar and comfortable with using it. You could also try to arrange a mock interview over Zoom.

What questions might be asked in 11 Plus interviews?

To do well in the interview, you child needs to be prepared to answer questions about:

- Themselves – interests, hobbies, academic achievements, etc.

- Their motivations for going to the school.

- Current affairs.

Candidates are often presented with a creative thinking task. For example, a child might be:

- Presented with two different pictures and asked to find a connection between the two and discuss it.

- Shown a piece of abstract art and be asked what they think it depicts and why the artist chose to depict it as they did.

- Presented with images or headlines from contemporary news and asked what they think about it, how they would solve the issue covered, or what they would have done differently to prevent it.

There is often a Maths or English challenge. This might involve:

- Asking children to solve a Year 6 level Maths problem (usually mental maths).

- Presenting students with a poem or short piece of prose to read and asking them to discuss the text with the interviewer. The interviewer will ask comprehension-style questions and expect some level of analysis.

The difficulty of these interview questions will vary depending on the school and how academic or competitive it is.

Remember, with most interview questions, especially creative ones, there is no right or wrong answer. The purpose of the question is to open up a discussion and to see how your child thinks and responds to being challenged. It is key to teach your child not to panic if they do not initially know what to say. Tell them it is OK to take a breath and think before answering. The interviewer would always prefer a thought-through answer over a rushed one.

Remind children that if the interviewer challenges them on their response, it does not mean they have said anything wrong. Instead, it is usually just an indication that they want to hear more from them and see how they adapt. It is fine for your child to change their mind, as long as they explain why.

How to prepare for success in interviews

11 Plus interviews aim to explore candidates' interests, academic character and personal qualities. The interview is a chance for them to get to know your child and determine if they will be a good fit at the school. Usually, the tone is friendly and relaxed, with the interviewer aiming to put your child at ease.

Most schools are looking for well-rounded children, so it is important your child has something to say when asked about their interests beyond academics. They can discuss anything that they are able to contribute to the school community, such as a passion in Music, Drama, sport, Art, debating or charity work.

Interviewers are looking for enthusiastic, confident children whom they will enjoy having at the school, and who will make the most of what the school has to offer.

To do well in the interview your child should be able to:

- Articulate themselves clearly and confidently.

- Answer the question given directly, rather than meandering around the point.

- Answer questions naturally and honestly – interviewers prefer not to have candidates who appear overpractised or give answers that seem rehearsed. Instead, they should be able to engage with the interviewer and respond naturally.

During their interview, children should avoid the following.

Giving one-word answers: Interviewers are aiming to see how well your child can communicate, so if they only answer in short sentences or single words, it will not reflect well on them. Children should respond in clear sentences and be able to expand on a point. When asked to discuss a specific topic (eg a favourite book, subject or hobby) they should aim to give two or three examples and explain their reasoning, although they must also be sure to balance talking with listening.

Fidgeting: Fidgeting can deter from your child's answers and will make them come across as anxious or distracted. You should try and work with your child to avoid playing with their hands or clothes and making repetitive motions as they speak. A little is fine and to be expected, however constant movement will divert attention from the conversation for both the child and interviewer. It is also important to maintain good eye contact.

Finally, remind your child to always smile and thank the interviewer at the end. Good manners matter.

Practice interviews

Interview technique is difficult for anyone, especially small children, so I highly recommend setting up one or two mock interviews a few weeks before the day itself. This will help your child hone their technique, get accustomed to the format, and build their confidence so they are less nervous on the day. If their first ever interview is an entrance interview, they may get thrown on the day and not perform as well as they could. If possible, set up a mock interview with a stranger to your child, such as an unfamiliar teacher or adult friend, so they are better prepared for the real thing. Some tutoring agencies will also offer mock interviews, or if you are having private tuition, you may be able to ask your tutor to help with this.

Remember, however, that it is not a good idea for your child to rehearse answers or overprepare. It is also important not to try and 'feed' your child answers. If they do not like sports, for instance, they shouldn't say that they do. Mock interviews are simply to help children get used to the format of interviews and to practise expressing themselves clearly.

You can also help your child prepare by having conversations together as a family during meals, or one-on-one when you have time together. This provides a great opportunity to develop the conversational skills that are central to good interview technique.

Interviews with shy or reserved children

Parents of shy or introverted children are often particularly concerned about the interview stage. They fear that it is an insurmountable hurdle for a reserved child to overcome, or that they must alter their child's personality, style or self-expression for the purpose of passing. This is not the case. While there are certain habits that introverted children might need to break to perform well in interviews, reticent children are otherwise not at a disadvantage and will not be overlooked or automatically rejected at the interview stage.

Indeed, many schools aim to make offers to a variety of personality types and therefore will not dismiss a child solely for being less loud or bubbly than their peers. As long as your child can hold a conversation and show passion and interest, it will not matter if they are not as extroverted as other candidates. This can even be an advantage, as overly extroverted children can come across as domineering or arrogant.

Nonetheless, there are certain elements of interview technique that all children must master so they can present themselves confidently:

- Maintaining good eye contact with the interviewer.

- Avoiding covering the mouth when talking.

- Speaking clearly and loudly enough for the interviewer to hear.

Past interview questions

Here I have compiled a list of some common interview questions. These can help you to conduct a mock interview or help to form the basis of a discussion with your child to help get them thinking and build their confidence in speaking.

1. What makes you special?

2. What is your favourite subject at school and why?

3. What is your favourite book and why?

4. What are you proud of?

5. What have you been up to this week?

6. What do you like about this school?

7. Would you rather come to school on an elephant or a giraffe and why?

8. Where would you park the elephant or giraffe? With the scooters?

9. Here is something we printed out on our 3D printer – what do you think it is?

10. Explain yellow to a blind person.

11. Explain kindness to an alien who speaks English.

12. What question would you like to ask the alien?

13. Who is your best friend and why?

14. What would they say about you?

15. What is your biggest weakness?

16. What is your greatest achievement?

17. What is the main thing affecting climate change?

18. What new subjects are you interested in taking up at secondary school?

19. What is one thing politicians are currently doing that you would change?

20. Aside from academics, what are you hoping to contribute to this school?

21. Are there any questions you would like to ask me?

22. What are you doing this weekend/later today?

Group assessments

Some schools organise group assessments as part of their interview stage, either in conjunction with them or instead of a traditional interview. Group assessments – also referred to as group discussions, creative assessment days, activity days and pre-selection assessments – generally involve problem-solving, creative tasks and larger interviews, in which candidates are split into small groups of anywhere between three and eight children.

Groups assessments are used by schools as a way to gauge candidates' creativity, problem-solving ability and teamwork skills. They are less conventional than interviews and have a far more varied structure, meaning they are generally more difficult to prepare for.

An example activity might be planning a survival trip. Candidates would be placed into groups of three with one teacher to observe them and help guide the discussion. They would be given a collection of items including bottled water, sun cream and a fishing rod, and then asked as a group to discuss which three resources to take and what must be left behind. Clearly there is no right or wrong answer, but the children will be asked to justify their choices and explain them as a group.

The main thing schools are looking to see in activities like this are:

- That a child can work collaboratively and involve others.

- That they know when to speak up and when to listen.

- That they can demonstrate respect for others, eg by building upon their contributions rather than only valuing their own.

- That they can share the stage and allow everyone to make a contribution.

The most important element of group assessments is teamwork. Candidates should make a conscious effort to co-operate with their group to achieve the best results. This can be difficult to teach your child, and sometimes the only way to learn is through experience. Gently remind them to be mindful of their peers and make sure everyone has an opportunity to speak, for instance around the dinner table or with their siblings.

It is important to hear from everyone in group assessments, so your child must make sure that they get a chance to speak and involve themselves in the process. It can be hard in some groups to avoid being steamrolled, but unfortunately, the teacher will not be able to provide any positive feedback if your child does not contribute anything. Equally, children should not speak over others in group assessments. No matter how much of a natural leader, or how good at the task your child is, if they do not give others an opportunity to contribute, they will not have succeeded in the assessment.

It is always important to remember that teachers will pick students that they want to teach. One of the primary benefits of group assessments over one-on-one interviews is they allow the teacher to observe how candidates interact with their peers. Your child should make an effort to be polite and kind to the other candidates. No matter how efficiently a child solves a problem, they will not receive positive feedback if they appear dismissive or mean towards other candidates – teachers will not want that behaviour in their classroom and will not reward it. But if your child is enthusiastic and positive about other candidates' contributions, they are much more likely to do well. It can be hard to remember that despite the feeling of competition with your peers in a group assessment, you should be working with them and not against them. Even if your child does not produce an idea themselves, if they are able to support the candidate who did and encourage them, that will be just as beneficial.

PART THREE
SUPPORTING YOUR CHILD

No matter how developed your child is on the academic scale, and in their maturity and sensitivity, they will need a lot of support to come through the 11 Plus process happy and relaxed. They will inevitably feel the pressure and expectation of the assessments and the lead-up to them; these will likely be the first tests they take where the outcome really matters to their lives. This part of *How to Pass the 11 Plus* covers all of the support available and how you can best help your child.

NINE

The Role Of Tuition

Parents who have made the decision to send a child to a secondary school with a selective entrance exam naturally want to know how to best support their child through the requisite tests and interviews. Although schools tend to discourage private tuition, the question of whether or not to engage a tutor is likely to cross your mind. This is especially the case when school gate chat or local parent forums begin to buzz with the names of mysterious tutors with two-year waiting lists and 'guaranteed' results.

This chapter will cut through the mystery and mythology surrounding private tuition and help you decide if your child needs a tutor, what your options for tuition are, and how intensely you should tutor your child.

How can a tutor help my child?

If your child is already extremely academic and capable, you may well wonder if private tuition is necessary. The answer to this question depends on a variety of factors.

Is your child at a state or independent primary school?

As mentioned previously, state schools will not teach the entirety of the KS2 syllabus in English and Maths in time for the 11 Plus tests. Similarly, state schools do not teach reasoning skills or give time to reasoning practice in Years 4 and 5. Children who attend state primary schools also tend to have less experience of taking assessments and may not have developed the requisite skills in exam technique.

Parents of children at state schools therefore have the difficult task of bringing forward the teaching of the Year 6 syllabus to the summer holidays after Year 5 at the latest. They must also find a way to teach the Reasoning syllabus to their children and help them become familiar with the main types of Verbal and Non-verbal questions used in the entrance exams of their target schools.

In these instances, tutoring can be a good way of ensuring your child is up to speed with all the required elements of the 11 Plus examination, not to mention reducing your own workload as a parent.

Independent primary schools do teach the entire 11 Plus curriculum to students, but it can still be extremely valuable for students at independent schools to have the individual attention of a tutor. A tutor will help to identify your child's strengths and weaknesses and work to fill in the gaps to an individualised degree that is simply not possible in a classroom setting. Many tutors can also provide advice and training specific to certain schools and their exam processes, which again is not typically possible in a classroom setting.

Are you hoping to get an academic scholarship?

If you are interested in an academic scholarship you may wish to consider tuition. Scholarships are extremely competitive and tutoring will offer useful additional support (although of course there are no guarantees). For instance, a tutor can teach your child effective exam technique, meaning they reach the end of their exam paper with enough time to properly attempt the challenging scholarship questions.

What are your child's weaker areas?

Even if you do not engage a tutor from the start of your child's 11 Plus journey, it can be useful to bring one in once you have a clearer sense of your child's weaker areas. If they have good ability but are falling down on timing, you might wish to bring in a tutor to improve exam technique. Or, if your child is shy, a tutor might be useful for supporting interview preparation.

A word of warning

It is tempting for parents with the available funds to tutor their child intensely to get them into a competitive and highly academic school. If your child's academic potential suggests that they will be able to manage the demands of such a school, this is reasonable. But you must be realistic. Intensely tutoring a child to gain a place at a school that is too advanced for them will ultimately be unproductive and can have a disastrous impact on a child's experience of secondary education.

What are the benefits of tuition?

Less pressure on parents: The amount of work needed to help children prepare for the 11 Plus can be daunting and undeniably places a significant burden on parents. The experience and expertise of a tutor allow parents to take a step back from the direct preparation and pass some responsibility on to a trained professional. Although parents must still provide their child with support, a tutor will be better placed to help with things like knowledge of syllabus requirements and exam technique.

Remember, though, that tuition can place extra time pressure on your child. Before you engage a tutor, you must ensure your child has time to have the sessions and do the set homework alongside any other activities, such as musical instruments, sports – and time off! If they do not and their weeks are too busy, tuition can ultimately be counterproductive.

Individualised support: The individualised support that tutoring provides will undoubtedly boost your child's potential of success. A good tutor will get to know your child and tailor sessions to their particular academic needs and learning style. Tutors can also help to boost confidence and provide the encouragement your child may not be receiving in school.

Exam-specific preparation: To pass the 11 Plus, your child needs to understand the English and Maths syllabus, practise Verbal and Non-verbal Reasoning, take several mock exam papers to master exam technique and prepare for their interview. This requires sustained effort over time. A tutor familiar with the demands of the 11 Plus can help to devise an effective game plan for your child to ensure all the necessary work is done in advance of their examinations.

How much tuition does my child need?

How much tuition you should get for your child depends on both the individual and their target schools. You need to know the answers to the following questions:

- What is expected of applicants to your target schools?

- How much is your child's primary school teaching them?

- How well is your child currently performing in tests?

All of these factors should be considered when deciding how much tuition your child needs.

Most parents begin tutoring in January of Year 5 with around one hour a week. This might increase as the exam approaches, depending on how well your child is progressing and how much support they need.

School holidays offer a great opportunity for students to cover more of the required syllabus or to reinforce their learning from the previous term. Some parents choose to only have a tutor during the holidays to reduce pressure on their child in term time. Others send their children on holiday courses where students work on 11 Plus preparations in a small group setting. This can be a great option if you feel your child could use some help consolidating their knowledge, or if they are behind on some areas of content.

Tuition options

If you are considering tuition, it is important to investigate all the available options so you can make an informed decision on what will work best for you and your child.

Here are some of the options available to you:

Individual tuition

One-to-one tuition with an experienced tutor is the most typical format for tutoring. Individual tutoring allows the tutor to tailor lessons entirely to the child's needs so that they can receive the most useful content for them in the most beneficial way. Downsides of this method can be that students become over-reliant on the help of a tutor and are less independent learners.

Paired tuition

Many parents opt for their children to be tutored with a friend. This can be a great option if your child is shy, or if you are aiming to improve your child's attitude to school and learning, as it can make it more of a fun and social activity. Paired tutoring also promotes discussion and provides the opportunity for pupils to learn from each other. Finally, paired tuition can be a cheaper option if your tutor is willing to split the cost.

Group tutoring and holiday courses

Some companies offer group tutoring. This option is beneficial for children who learn better when surrounded by their peers. Learning in a small group with the same goals can help motivate children to do well and build their confidence as they work with others. Holiday courses offer similar benefits as they also provide a social learning environment. Many children respond well to having intensive workshop-style teaching over the course of a few days, but it is important to remember that this will mean your child receives less individual attention and the content of the course cannot be tailored as accurately to the exams they will be sitting.

What should I look for in a tutor?

If you choose to get an individual tutor, there are some things you will want to look out for:

- **How qualified are they?**

  Tuition from a fully qualified teacher will clearly be of higher quality than tuition from a sixth form student, but their price will also reflect this, and a teaching qualification certainly isn't a prerequisite for good tuition. Consider other factors, such as how many hours of tutoring experience they have, how many children have they successfully tutored through the 11 Plus, and what their success rate is at your target schools.

- **What is their specialism?**

  It is wise to employ a tutor who specialises in the particular areas your child needs help in, whether that is the 11 Plus generally or the particular subject, eg Maths, that your child struggles in.

- **Do they have experience with your target schools?**

  You may wish to engage a tutor with specific experience and a good track record of getting students into your target schools. Again, pricing is likely to be higher for these tutors, but if you are able to pay the extra cost, it will be worth it.

- **Can they provide a DBS certificate and references/testimonials?**

  As a matter of safeguarding, tutors should be able to provide an enhanced DBS certificate and references from previous clients.

- **What is their teaching style?**

  A good tutor will teach students exactly what they need to know to pass the exam, with methods that they find effective and engaging. I recommend finding a tutor who is committed to making learning dynamic and fun for students, and who will not overwhelm or overwork them. From a personality perspective, you want to find someone your child can build a rapport with, but who will also be honest with you about your child's progress.

Tuition agencies

One way to find a qualified and experienced tutor who meets your needs is to use a tuition agency. A tuition agency can be an invaluable tool in your 11 Plus armoury. From the beginning of your 11 Plus journey, they can offer an academic assessment, personalised advice on choosing schools, summer courses and mock exams, and, of course, bespoke tutoring services.

An agency will have a vast bank of expert tutors with whom they can pair your child according to your needs. Not only will this give you access to highly capable tutors for each area of the 11 Plus, but it will also allow you to quickly find an alternative option if you are not happy with your tutor. Another benefit of using an agency is that they will have pre-screened all their tutors, meaning there is less to worry about checking from your end.

TEN

Scholarships

Most independent secondary schools offer academic scholarships to their most high-achieving applicants. Many also offer Sport and Music scholarships, while a smaller portion offer scholarships in Art, Drama, and Design and Technology. Some offer all-rounder scholarships for those who excel in two or more areas.

A scholar will usually receive a monetary award, although this is often small, and the benefit is expressed more in terms of prestige than financial value. Many schools offer non-academic scholarship prizes related to the subject in question – for example, a Music scholar might receive free lessons in an instrument of their choice, or a Sports scholar might receive free kit. This may be instead of or in addition to a monetary award.

Scholars will be expected to actively participate in their skill in the school community. This will include attending extra-curricular activities, excelling in lessons and usually taking the subject up to at least GCSE level. If the scholar fails to meet the standard upheld by the school, they may have their scholarship revoked.

It is worth noting that scholars are expected to participate in ongoing enhancement programmes pertaining to their area of award once they start at the school. For this reason, you should only put your child forward for a scholarship if they are genuinely passionate about the subject or subjects in question.

How do candidates apply for a scholarship?

At most schools, every applicant who sits the entrance exam is automatically eligible for an academic scholarship. However, at others, parents need to apply for their child to be considered for an academic scholarship.

For non-academic scholarships, you will need to apply specifically. There is usually a section in the general school application where you can say you are planning to submit a scholarship application. The school will then contact you with the requirements and ask you fill in a specific application form and/or submit evidence and paperwork. As always, it is a good idea to check the specific application process and requirements of your target schools.

Note that references will typically be requested to support your scholarship application, so before checking the box, it is sensible to check that the person in question (for instance, your child's hockey coach or their Head of Music) will be happy to support the application. Also ensure that whoever is writing your child's general reference is aware that you have applied for a scholarship so that they can mention this.

Academic scholarships

How do you know if your child is a suitable candidate for an academic scholarship?

Schools pitch their academic levels differently and this applies for their scholarship cohorts too. A child who achieves a scholarship at one school may not be in the running for a scholarship at another. To gain a scholarship at a selective school, your child must perform at a very high standard.

What is the process for achieving an academic scholarship?

The process varies by school. However, typically the standard exam is taken and the top 10 to 20% of the candidates offered a place are either also offered a scholarship or invited back for a scholarship interview (or interviews). There are often a few questions at the back of the exam which are, in effect, the scholarship questions. Candidates would therefore only get the requisite score if they got far enough into the exam and did well on these questions. This means that speed and accuracy on the more routine parts of the exam are key to achieving an academic scholarship.

While some schools offer a scholarship purely based on the exam, others invite students to a scholarship interview. The questions asked in these are likely to be harder than standard interview questions and students need to be well-prepared if they are to succeed. For instance, they might be asked advanced mental maths questions or to analyse an unseen piece of literature.

Tips for the Maths paper

Scholarships are won in the Maths paper by successfully tackling the hard questions in the final quarter of the paper. These questions are specifically chosen to ensure no children have seen them before or have had an opportunity to practise them. Children hoping to score well need to ensure they:

- Move speedily and accurately through the first sections of the paper, leaving enough time to tackle scholarship questions.
- Practise how to approach all sorts of mathematical problems and feel confident to do so.

- Be prepared to tackle more advanced material than they may have studied at school.

- Be able to record their workings to demonstrate how they have tackled the problem.

Tips for the English paper

Scholarships are normally won on the English paper by demonstrating advanced comprehension skills and the ability to explain and use sophisticated narrative techniques. For example, scholars need to understand how and why authors might create certain effects, beyond the standard use of metaphors or similes.

Scholars will be expected to write a superb creative piece, using appropriate yet advanced vocabulary, excellent syntax and flow, and flawless grammar and spelling. Their stories should be imaginative, well structured, and clear.

Non-academic scholarships

How do you know if your child is a suitable candidate for a non-academic scholarship?

If your child is applying for a non-academic scholarship, it is essential that they are enthusiastic about the subject in question, willing to put in the extra work that is required, and capable of meeting the school's scholarship criteria.

What is the process for achieving a non-academic scholarship?

The process varies from school to school, so as ever, the most important thing is to do your research. Find out what standard is expected of scholars at your target schools and what the selection process involves. This will allow you to hone your preparation and will give your child the greatest chance of success.

There is usually a section on the general school application that will allow you to opt in for consideration for a scholarship in, say, Sport or Art. These usually have certain requirements (eg a particular grade level in Music), and schools may also ask you to submit videos of your child performing or practising their specialist skill. Art or DT scholarship candidates are usually required to submit a portfolio. There is then a screening process, and the most promising candidates are likely to be invited to the school for an in-person assessment. For a prospective Sports scholar, this will involve playing a range of different sports with other candidates in front of teachers. A Music candidate will be expected to perform a prepared piece of music on their chosen instrument(s), sight read, and possibly sing. Drama scholars will be asked to prepare and perform two or more pieces.

The audition or try-out will sometimes be followed by a scholarship interview, usually conducted by the relevant Head of Department. This will be in addition to the general interview but requires specific preparation. Your child will be asked questions related to their subject and will be expected to express themselves confidently and clearly while displaying passion and commitment.

Bursaries

Unlike scholarships, bursaries are awarded by independent schools on the basis of financial need. A bursary does not necessarily mean a discount of 100% however – they will often be partial. It is also important to bear in mind that the hidden costs of a private school education, such as uniform, school trips, and technology, which may not be covered by a bursary.

Parents should note that bursaries are generally means-tested on a yearly basis. If financial circumstances change, a bursary may no longer be available. This can go both ways – a parent whose child is already attending a school without a bursary can usually apply for a bursary in the subsequent year if necessary.

What is the process of applying for a bursary?

In most cases, parents can apply for a bursary during the initial application process. Bursaries tend to be highly competitive and are usually offered to only the highest performing children who also meet the financial requirements. It is important for parents planning to apply for bursaries to be aware that they will need to submit themselves to high levels of financial disclosure as part of the application process.

Although bursary schemes vary widely, they are more common than many imagine. In fact, one in three students at independent schools have some degree of fee assistance.[10] It is a good idea to get in contact with the schools you are interested in to get a proper sense of their bursary offerings. The details of bursaries may not be clearly advertised on the website, and in some cases there may be specific bursaries available, so it is best to ask directly so that you can ascertain what might be possible for you and your child.

---

10 C Calkin, 'Can you afford the growing cost of school fees?' (*Financial Times*, 2021) www.ft.com/content/8ff9f608-f310-453e-bfbd -68d12d00a9e1, accessed 14 February 2022

ELEVEN

Supporting Your Child's Wellbeing

The 11 Plus can place a great deal of pressure on children. It is important to be aware of this and to manage your child's mental and physical wellbeing throughout the 11 Plus process to ensure that their academic performance is not negatively affected.

The school application process can be demanding on parents. It is essential that you keep an eye on your own stress levels and that you are careful not to pass any anxiety on to your children. Many of the wellbeing tips included below are applicable to adults, and you might want to incorporate some of them into your own life. Indeed, engaging in activities like mindfulness or sports with your child can be a great way of spending relaxing quality time together.

Why is wellbeing important?

Research conducted by the Department of Education into the importance of pupil wellbeing found that:

- Children with better emotional wellbeing make more progress in primary school and are more engaged in secondary school.

- Children with better attention skills experience greater progress across the four Key Stages of schooling in England.

- Children who are physically active – particularly in terms of playing team sports – are more likely to be successful both during and after their time at school. All forms of exercise have been shown to improve brain function, build self-confidence, and improve work ethic.[11]

These findings indicate the concrete benefits that supporting your child's wellbeing in a holistic manner can have on their academic performance.

There are two key pillars of wellbeing: emotional and physical. In this chapter, we will discuss why they are so important and I'll give tips on how you can support

---

11 Leslie Morrison Gutman and John Verhaus, 'The impact of pupil behaviour and wellbeing on educational outcomes' (Childhood Wellbeing Research Centre, 2012) https://assets.publishing.service.gov.uk/government/uploads/system/uploads/attachment_data/file/219638/DFE-RR253.pdf, accessed 23 December 2021

your child in each area. I also suggest ways you can improve your child's wellbeing during periods of exam preparation by making learning fun.

Emotional wellbeing

In the modern world, children face varied challenges and can often feel pressure from multiple sources. Mental health issues in children are unfortunately on the rise, and with this in mind, it is more important than ever that parents recognise the importance of emotional wellbeing, particularly during stressful periods such as exam season.

As well as affecting their day-to-day life, poor emotional health is linked to worse outcomes later in life, such as reduced academic achievement and employment prospects.[12]

By contrast, a strong sense of emotional wellbeing has been found to help students:

- Develop a positive relationship with learning

- Resist peer pressure

- Increase their self-awareness

---

12 World Health Organization, 'Adolescent mental health' (World Health Organization, 2021) www.who.int/news-room/fact-sheets /detail/adolescent-mental-health, accessed 23 December 2021

- Build resilience
- Cope with strong feelings and manage their behaviour
- Develop a positive relationship with themselves
- Improve communication skills

How to support your child's emotional wellbeing

Emotional wellbeing is influenced by a wide range of complex factors, but parents can undoubtedly play a crucial role. Here are some ways you can help your child.

Practise mindfulness: Mindfulness has gained a lot of attention over recent years, and rightly so. It can have powerful effects on mood and wellbeing. Regular mindfulness practice has been shown to help children:

- Improve focus
- Develop healthy coping mechanisms
- Self-regulate negative or overwhelming emotions
- Reduce stress and anxiety

There are lots of different mindfulness techniques for you and your child to experiment with, including meditation, counting breaths, and even reciting mantras. The aim is to help your child feel calm, present and fully connected to their body. There are plenty of mindfulness resources available online, such as the Calm and Headspace apps and the Positive Psychology website.

Try breathing exercises: Learning how to regulate the breath at times of stress or anxiety is a useful technique for children to develop. When we experience something unexpected or shocking, our heart rate increases, digestion slows, and the breath becomes rapid and shallow. Children can find this physical state frightening, and this will only exacerbate any negative emotions they are experiencing, so it is important to show them how to reset. Deep breathing does this by helping to get more oxygen into the bloodstream, instantly calming the body and relieving any stress or tension that they might be feeling.

Create a happiness jar: If your child tends to dwell on the negative things in life, then a happiness jar can help them to adopt a more positive outlook. Ask your child to think about a few happy moments from the week or the day, discuss them together, and then jot each moment down on a piece of paper and place them in an empty jar. The simple act of remembering these positive moments will give your child a greater appreciation of how much they have to be grateful for, and hopefully of how much other people value them. Best of all, the jar is always there. If your child is ever feeling down, you can look through some of the comments together to boost their mood.

Encourage them to switch off (and follow suit!): While it is probably unrealistic to expect your child to totally switch off from their devices, encourage them to take breaks and have extended periods of time away from the internet, their phone, or the TV each evening. Research shows that too much time spent staring at a screen can be bad for children's sense of wellbeing,[13] and has even been connected to worse academic performance.[14]

The best way to help your children relax and switch off is to lead by example. Put your own device away and insist on digital blackouts for the whole family at various times – when you are having your evening meal, for example.

Physical wellbeing

The link between body and mind is well documented: simply put, good physical health leads to a better quality of life, increased engagement – both socially and academically – and enhanced productivity. In addition, children who exercise regularly, eat well, and sleep

---

13 Victoria Zamperoni, 'Screen time and children's mental health: what does the evidence say?' (Mental Health Foundation, 2018) www .mentalhealth.org.uk/blog/screen-time-and-childrens-mental -health-what-does-evidence-say, accessed 23 December 2021

14 Jennifer Cross, 'What does too much screen time do to children's brains?' (Health Matters, NewYork-Presbyterian, 2021) https:// healthmatters.nyp.org/what-does-too-much-screen-time-do-to -childrens-brains, accessed 23 December 2021

the recommended amount are more likely to perform better at school.

Physical activity has been proven to:

- Enlarge the part of the brain that controls our ability to concentrate and focus.

- Stimulate the release of 'feel-good' chemicals like serotonin, which helps to boost both mood and energy levels. This is especially true when combined with mental activity and socialisation, for instance when playing a team sport.

- Promote good overall health and wellbeing, for instance by reducing the risk of obesity.

- Improve sleep, which in turn helps to boost concentration and mood.

- Lower stress levels and help to combat anxiety and other mental health struggles.[15]

Be a role model

Try to be a role model for your children by making regular exercise and a diet of healthy, nourishing foods a solid part of your lifestyle. The example set by parents at an early age can have a real impact on children's long-term health prospects. If you introduce your child

---

15 Better Health, 'Healthier families: Activities' (NHS UK, no date) www.nhs.uk/change4life/activities, accessed 23 December 2021

to a wide variety of wholesome foods at an early age, they are more likely to appreciate the tastes of healthy, fresh produce into adulthood. Similarly, if regular exercise is a part of your family's routine, then your children are more far more likely to keep up the habit as they get older.

While your children should be encouraged to make healthy decisions for themselves, during their younger years they will rely on your guidance and support. That means monitoring what they eat, how much exercise they get and how much time they spend being sedentary, and trying to encourage healthy choices as much as possible.

Wellbeing is important at every stage in your child's life, but it is especially vital during stressful periods such as exam season. Ironically, this is often the time when healthy habits can slip. Ensure that you continue to encourage your child to take enough time away from work to exercise, sleep and relax and that you do not become overly reliant on treats like chocolate and sweets as incentives.

The role of the family

Undergoing the long process of the 11 Plus can be challenging for families, but it is vital to maintain a sense of perspective and ensure that the family environment remains stress-free. Even as pressure mounts, it is important not to let regular family activities fall by the wayside as these help children to decompress, which will support their chances of success in the long run. Communal activities such as playing games, reading together, watching films, or simply eating dinner as a family all help to contribute to a happy and healthy home life, which in turn will support your child's wellbeing.

It is also important to avoid making every conversation you have with your child in the run-up to the exams about the 11 Plus. While it can be difficult to take your mind off the exam, it is vital to give your child a reprieve and to avoid putting excess pressure on them.

Finally, it is vital that you do not let any anxiety you may be feeling about the 11 Plus affect your child. Although you may occasionally feel stressed or worried, do not show or tell your child about your fears, as it will likely transfer onto them. Children should not feel they are responsible for your stress, or that it is their job to reduce your stress. Your child should only be focussing on the work they are doing and not be burdened by unnecessary anxiety that might hinder their preparation and performance.

Preparing for the results

Ensuring you and your child are prepared for both success and failure in the 11 Plus is essential. As you will be aware by this stage in the book, the 11 Plus is a considerable undertaking, and the end of the process can be highly emotional. Preparing your child in advance for receiving the big news will help reduce some of the stress surrounding results day.

It is possible for children to become very anxious about 11 Plus results. To mitigate this, try to reduce some of the pressure surrounding the process. You want to avoid a situation where your child has tied their self-worth or self-esteem to these results, or where they feel that your affection as a parent depends on how well they do. This is not to deny the importance of the exams, but merely to emphasise the value of maintaining perspective, even if the results are not what you had hoped.

I recommend framing the 11 Plus as a learning experience. For instance, you could talk about how useful the process of taking a public exam or having a formal interview for the first time will be for them later in life. Present the sitting of the exam as the main achievement, rather than focussing entirely on the results. Preparing for extremely demanding exams, attending interviews, and sitting challenging papers are all achievements in and of themselves and should be treated as such. Make sure you reward or congratulate your child after every stage of the process – even if they feel they have done badly. 'The taking part is what counts' should be your mantra.

Use positive language throughout the 11 Plus process. Reiterate to your child that you are only interested in them doing their best, and that you are hugely proud of them no matter what happens. Remind your child that the 11 Plus is a challenging process, and that they should not be disappointed if they do not receive offers from every school that they apply to.

As a parent, you also need to be prepared for results day. Do not treat any of the schools you apply to as a safe bet. The 11 Plus is highly competitive and unfortunately things can go wrong on the day, even at schools you might have considered an 'insurance'. You do not want any disappointment to be visible to your child, so make sure you prepare for every scenario. If things do not go to plan, the most important thing is that you are ready to comfort your child and that you have a strategy in place for next steps.

In the next part of the book, we'll go into more detail on what happens after your child has completed the 11 Plus process, including what to do if things do not go to plan.

PART FOUR
RESULTS DAY
AND BEYOND

Parents rightly focus on the 11 Plus assessment days themselves, but there is always a period after the exams when you will be waiting for invitations to further rounds, interviews and then offer letters. This can be an anxious time for you and your child. There will be gossip and rumours at the school gates and the wait can seem interminable. Once your child has their place, they may suddenly be struck with nerves about leaving their small primary school and heading to big school. They may be upset about leaving friends and worried about finding their way to their new school and around a big site. We deal with all these issues in the next chapters.

TWELVE

The Results

After the busy rush of the 11 Plus, the period after all the examinations and interviews are over can be anxiety-provoking for both parents and children. This is natural – but remember that worrying won't make the results come any sooner.

When the news does arrive, it could contain:

- An immediate offer

- An offer of a place on the waiting list

- A 'no offer' letter

In this chapter, we'll discuss each of these possibilities in more detail.

Immediate offers

First and foremost, say a huge well done to your child! Tell them how proud you are of them and remind them of all the exciting things about the school they have been offered a place at. This is especially important if they didn't get an offer at their first-choice school. But even if they do, it is worth discussing, as the open days will probably feel like a distant memory.

Most schools will give you the option to visit again before you accept the offer. This can be a good idea, especially if your child has received multiple offers and doesn't have a firm favourite. Even if they only receive one offer it can be nice to visit the school again to get your child excited about starting there.

If your child receives multiple offers, try not to delay letting the schools know your decision. Sitting on multiple offers unnecessarily means children on the waiting list will be left in limbo.

Waiting lists

A place on the waiting list means that, although the school feels your child would be a good fit, there were stronger candidates. As schools can only send out a limited number of offers, the waiting list allows them to fill places with strong candidates if some of the children they send immediate offers to decline a place at the school. Although receiving a waiting list offer can be frustrating and stressful, it is important not to let your child see this. Remember how competitive the 11 Plus process is. It is very impressive to receive a waiting list offer, and you should make your child aware of this.

If your child receives a waiting list offer you must contact the school immediately to confirm that you wish to be kept on the list. A short, polite email or quick phone call will suffice. If the school is your first choice and you would be prepared to accept the place as soon as it is offered, then it is worth letting them know that. But don't promise to immediately accept an offer if you are not prepared to do so. Remember that it will be a very busy period for school registrars. Although it is fine to stay in contact with them, you need to get the tone right. Be polite but understanding – a demanding attitude won't do your child any favours.

Frustratingly, waiting list places sometimes only convert into offers at the very last minute. This is because families who receive immediate offers can be slow to respond. Sometimes they are also waiting to hear about waiting list offers! Try to hold your nerve and don't give up hope.

No offers

If your child receives disappointing news, try not to panic. Things can still change up to the last minute due to families changing their minds, relocating or accepting offers at other schools. Speak to your child's school to get their advice. They may be able to assist you with making enquiries at other schools and are likely to have a good sense of which schools still have available places.

If your child has been rejected by a grammar school, you also have the option of appealing the decision. This is a complicated process and by no means guarantees that the decision will be reversed. For this reason, it is vital that your child accepts a place at whichever school they have been admitted to, even if you plan to launch an appeal.

There are three main instances when an appeal will be heard:

1. A school has failed to correctly follow the admissions process.

2. Your child has failed the 11 Plus exam, but there is sufficient evidence to prove that they meet the school's required academic standard.

3. There is proof that not attending the school in question will put your child at harm (eg due to family circumstances, special educational needs, mental health issues, bullying, travel issues, and so on).

In each case, you will need to provide considerable evidence for your appeal to be admitted and to pass to the next stage of the appeals process. The more evidence you can provide, the more likely your case will be successful, but the type of evidence you offer needs to be relevant to the basis of your appeal. A scattergun approach will not work in your favour. For instance, if you are appealing on the basis that your child does in fact meet the required academic standards of the school, you should provide school reports, references, previous exam scores (eg from school tests or mock exams), marked schoolwork and any awards or other evidence of their excellence.

The appeals process will depend on the school in question. Some schools make the decision internally, whereas others require you to submit evidence to the local authority. Information on the appeals process should be included with the paperwork notifying you of the school's decision. Make note of the deadlines and the evidence that you are likely to need to support your case.

If your initial case is accepted, you will be invited to a short hearing in front of a panel to present further evidence. After this, you should find out the decision within a week. This decision is final, but do not despair if your appeal is unsuccessful. If your child is on a waiting list, they may still gain a place before September.

Whatever happens, the most important thing is to congratulate your child on all the hard work they have done. Do not let any disappointment or concern that you may feel affect them as this would be far more damaging than them not getting into their first-choice school. Ultimately, a supportive family environment is equally important as the secondary school your child attends.

THIRTEEN

Starting Secondary School

While it might be hard to imagine at this stage in your journey, one day all the hard work of the 11 Plus will be over and your child will be starting at a great new school with all the exciting possibilities that entails. Starting a new school can provoke some anxiety, so in this chapter, I'll provide plenty of advice on making the transition to secondary school as smooth as possible.

How to prepare for starting secondary school

Look around the school again

It is important to help your child feel confident and comfortable on their first day. If possible, visit the school again so that your child feels familiar with their new environment before starting in September. Many schools will offer welcome events in the Summer term of Year 6. These are a great chance for your child to meet some of their new classmates and teachers before the first day.

Go shopping for school supplies

The school will send a list of the things your child needs at some point over the summer holiday (such as uniform, sports kit, stationery, and so on). It is important to make sure that you purchase all the items from the list, but this can also be a great opportunity to indulge in some retail therapy with your child and to help make the prospect of returning to the classroom a fun one. Allowing them to choose a colourful notebook, a cool pencil case or some brightly coloured pens will make the process more enjoyable and help to get them excited about school.

Jot down important dates and a potential school schedule

You will also receive the school calendar during the summer holidays. As obvious as it may sound, it is worth highlighting any important dates and making sure these are all listed in your own diary – things will get busy as the term progresses, and this way you can feel confident that you will not miss anything.

It can also be useful to spend some time thinking about schedules and priorities. For instance, when is your child going to do their homework in the evening – before or after dinner? If there are sports to be played or instruments to be practised, where do these fall in the pecking order? How much television or internet access will your child be allowed on a school night? Do all their other chores have to be finished first, or do you prefer to allow them some relaxation time immediately after school? There is no right or wrong answer, but it is important to discuss priorities with your child and set some guidelines. This will help ensure that the school year gets off to a flying start from the very first day.

Ease in to the routine

While a consistent routine is always important for children whether they are at school or not, it is easy for things to slip during the holidays. It is essential that the return to the classroom is not too much of a shock to the system, so I recommend starting to ease your child back in to a gentle routine before their first week back at school. Following this advice will not only help your child ease back into school without too much difficulty, but also will ensure that you avoid first-day mayhem.

Start by resetting sleep patterns to where they need to be during term time. Gradually introduce early nights – say, by bringing bedtime forward by half an hour each evening – until your child is going to bed and waking up at the appropriate times. Make sure you reach this point at least three days before school begins, so that your child is used to the new sleeping arrangement.

The same goes for eating habits, which need to be 'reset' so that your child maintains a good level of energy and focus throughout the school day. Wean the student in question off any bad habits – grazing all day, for instance – and impose a stricter regime of breakfast, lunch and dinner at set times, including some healthy snacks in between meals if necessary.

In terms of academic work, try to keep your child engaged and stimulated before they start secondary school. For instance, you could encourage them to read more challenging books over the summer, or to complete a fun project related to Maths, Science or History. Some schools will provide their own reading list for children to make a start on over the holidays.

Practise the school run

Primary school children are usually taken to school by their parents. Of course, it is up to you as parents to decide whether you feel your child is ready to start travelling independently. Consider things such as the length of the journey, the safety of the route your child will be taking, and their own maturity and confidence. If possible, you may want to arrange for them to travel to school with local friends, which can be a good way of transitioning into solo travel.

If you do decide that your child is ready to travel to school independently, I strongly recommend using the summer before they start at their new school to set up several trial runs of the journey. Your child will then be able to gradually build up their independence and will feel confident and prepared for the solo school run come September.

To relieve the anxiety you might feel about your child's journey to school, make sure to ask your child to text you when they have arrived safely at school or are starting the journey home. If you worry that your child will not remember to do this, you can download an app such as Find My Friends or Life360 so you can see their location.

I also suggest your child keeps emergency phone numbers in their bag in case they lose their phone and need to contact you. It is important to remember that while this new step may be daunting, it is a necessary step in growing up and gaining important skills like responsibility, timekeeping and self-sufficiency.

How to survive the first term

The move from primary to secondary school brings with it a significant expectation to do with independence: perhaps for the first time, your little one will be expected to behave more like a grown-up. This can be intimidating for some children, especially if they are young for their year. Be aware of these challenges and make sure you keep an eye on your child's emotional wellbeing, especially in the first term.

Build confidence

One daunting aspect of the transition to secondary school is that 'big' kids are suddenly small again: they have gone from being the oldest children in the school to being the 'newbies', surrounded by children older, and much bigger, than themselves. The school itself is also likely to be larger than their primary school, which can be overwhelming.

Helping your child gain confidence before they join their new school is the best way to combat any fears they might have. Maybe you can enrol them in a summer camp or weekend course so that they get used to meeting new people and operating in different environments. Before the first day itself, remind your child that everyone is in the same boat when they start. They will all feel nervous, and this is a perfectly natural and understandable feeling. If your child is particularly anxious, you may want to seek advice from an experienced adult like a teacher, or tutor, or better yet, an older child who has been through it already.

Talk to your child about friendships

At primary school, your child probably had some secure, established friendships and knew all the children in their year. But at their new school they might only know a few children or not know anyone and so may be feeling nervous about making new friends. To quell some of these worries, remind your child that friendships take time to develop and do not happen overnight. Reassure them not to panic if they have not made a friend instantly. A great way to make friends in Year 7 is to join a club or team so they can meet new children based on shared interests in other forms and year groups.

Your child may initially want to stick close to any friends from their primary school. While this is understandable, you should encourage them to get to know the new children in their class. Making new friends is a core part of Year 7 and they are sure to feel a lot more comfortable and happy at their new school when they have branched out and solidified friendships.

While the prospect of making new friends can be daunting, it should also be exciting! Secondary school gives your child an amazing opportunity to foster new connections, so although they may be nervous, remind them that this is a wonderful position to be in (and that everyone is in the same boat).

Encourage organisation

Children entering secondary school will be expected to take more responsibility for organising themselves and should be prepared for this. Staying organised is easy when done in small steps. Get your child to look at their timetable each evening and think about what they need for each lesson. Do not be tempted to pack their school bag for them – it is much better for them to get used to taking on this responsibility for themselves. Although it is a good idea to check in with your child regularly and remind them of anything they may have forgotten, the sooner they get used to taking on responsibility for themselves, the better. Many children find that they enjoy the sense of independence that comes from this.

In terms of staying on top of homework, you can help your child with this by setting up a homework planner and marking deadlines in it together with brightly coloured pens. This, together with a clear routine and a quiet space to work in, will make a big difference. Consider purchasing a whiteboard and hanging this near their desk, too – they can use this to post reminders and create a to-do list, which will help them stay on track of their work.

Keep an eye on their workload

Your child's workload will increase as they enter secondary school, and this can be a shock to the system. Help them to stay organised and make sure you regularly check in with them to see how they are coping.

If your child does not seem to settle, or is struggling with the work, do not panic. It could be that they just need more time to adjust. If you are still concerned about their work or their mood after a few weeks, talk to your child to see if you can find out what the reason is. If you do not think you can help them, make an appointment to discuss matters with their form tutor. They will be used to issues such as this and will be able to provide additional support. The sooner you do this the better.

Mobile phones and social media

Children often receive a smartphone when they start secondary school and usually have their first encounters with social media at this point too. Rather than burying your head in the sand or attempting to ban your child from using the internet, provide them with support, such as by setting up safe privacy settings, and talk with them about how to use the internet, mobile phones and social media responsibly.

Here are some of the things you can do if you're setting up a new mobile phone for your child:

- Set parental controls on your home broadband to prevent your child from seeing adult content while at home.
- Check that parental controls are set up on your child's mobile network.

- Use the device settings so they can only download age-appropriate apps and games.

- Set up password controls or disable in-app purchasing so that your child does not run up big bills accidentally.

- Check your child's profile and policy settings on any social media apps, making sure they are not sharing personal or private information with people they do not know.

Here are some things you can do to encourage responsible mobile phone usage:

- Tell your child that they should not accept friend requests from people or numbers they do not recognise.

- Enforce good habits around screen time, eg not having their phone in their room at night and having a break from their phone before they go to bed.

- Show your child how they can turn off notifications when they want to switch off and relax.

- Encourage them to let you know if they think bullying is happening online to themselves or other children. Importantly, make sure you react calmly and constructively if they do share any bad online behaviour so that they know they can trust you not to overreact.

Remember to build in time for healthy habits and relaxation. As the busy school year begins and the week fills up with homework and extra-curricular activities, it can be easy for good habits to slip. Try to make sure your child keeps up any hobbies they enjoy (whether that is reading, chess, dance – whatever helps them to relax) and still has plenty of time to see their friends, get fresh air and exercise, and sleep. Maintaining these healthy habits should help your child to approach school with a positive mindset and to make the most of all that it has to offer.

Conclusion

At Mentor Education, we have more than forty years' experience of guiding children and parents through the 11 Plus process. We know how intimidating the prospect of the 11 Plus can be and how shrouded in mystery the 'secrets to success' often appear. Not every parent is able to seek out the advice of a tuition company and so I wrote this book to demystify the 11 Plus and share with you the tips and tools that you need to maximise your child's chances of success. We give this advice on a daily basis to the parents who come in and see us, and having reached this point in the book, you are armed with the same knowledge about the things you need to tackle the 11 Plus process with confidence.

I have emphasised several key points throughout this book that, as we reach the end, it is worth highlighting again.

First, it is important to choose the right school for your child. You must balance ambition with realism when selecting a range of target schools for your child and make sure that their voice is heard throughout the decision-making process. Sending your child to a school that does not suit them will undoubtedly lead to future problems. It is worth investing the time to ensure that you have a strong selection of target schools, all of which you would be happy for your child to attend – and which they would be happy to go to.

Once you have chosen your target schools, it is essential that you pay close attention to each school's admissions process. As you will have realised, the 11 Plus is not one thing, but rather a process with multiple variations that depend on the school in question. You must know well in advance of beginning 11 Plus preparation the type of assessment that your child will be facing, from the admissions timeline, to the exam board, to the style of interview. Doing this research early on is a surefire way to maximise your child's chances of success.

Next, you will need a long-term 11 Plus strategy. A strong grasp of the syllabus, excellent exam technique, and confidence in their own ability are not things that your child can develop in a last-minute rush. It is vital that you take the long view on 11 Plus preparations, and plan backwards from the date of your child's exams to ensure they have ample time to prepare. Following our twelve-month programme will assist you with this, but as always, it is vital that you adapt our suggestions to the demands of your child's target schools.

Finally, although it is true that your child will need to put in a lot of work to do well in the 11 Plus, it is important that the preparation process does not become overly stressful. Not only is this likely to hamper your child's performance, but the long-term consequences of placing excess pressure on your child to succeed can be huge. The emotional and physical wellbeing of your child should always be the top priority, and you should factor this in to every stage of the 11 Plus process, from choosing a school, to preparing for the assessments, to the exam day itself. As we have frequently emphasised, it is also vital for you as parents to manage your own emotions and expectations, and to prevent any anxiety that you may feel from rubbing off onto your child.

The 11 Plus is undoubtedly a significant moment in your child's school career. But with this book at your side, it does not have to be something to fear. The advice I have set out in these pages has been honed over years of guiding students through the 11 Plus and tried and tested by the hundreds of families who come through our doors each year. It will give you access to our expertise at any time, help you support your child through every stage of the 11 Plus process, and give them the very best chance of success while keeping stress to a minimum. Through this book, I will be with you every step of the way. Good luck!

Resources

Resources for exam practice

Online resources

Atom – Atom Learning is an excellent adaptive online home learning platform for children ages seven to twelve and up. They offer content for each element of the written 11 Plus exam, unlimited practice tests tailored to your child's examination requirements, progress reports, and even live lessons.

Atom Learning Ltd, https://atomlearning.co.uk

Fun Learning – The Fun Learning website has some great games to develop critical thinking skills and reasoning in children.

Fun Learning, www.funlearning.co.uk

Planet BOFA – Planet BOFA is a personalised learning platform which tests, teaches, retests and tracks students' progress and helps to improve their learning by offering a 'laser-focus' on weaker areas.

Planet BOFA, www.bofa11plus.com

Education Quizzes – Education Quizzes is a popular website designed to help children consolidate their schoolwork. It is based on the simple concept that if learning is fun, children will be more enthusiastic about doing it. The content on the site is based on the national curriculum, so you can be sure your child is learning the correct material, and having fun while they do it.

Education Quizzes, www.educationquizzes.com

Study guides

Galore Books – Galore Books offer revision guides, workbooks and practice papers for each 11 Plus subject. They also provide a useful 'Study Skills' guide for students in Year 5 and 6.

Bond Books – Bond offer handbooks on each element of the 11 Plus examination, as well as question papers and test books to practise with.

CGP Books – CGP provide a variety of excellent 11 Plus resources, including study books, practice books, ten-minute tests and practice test papers. They offer options for both the GL and CEM test.

Reading suggestions

Throughout this handbook, we have emphasised the importance of regular reading for children's development, wellbeing and academic performance. Below is an extensive list of books suited to children between Years 5 and 6, which can help you get your child started on their reading journey.

Fiction

- *Rebound* by Kwame Alexander (Andersen Press, 2018)

- *Skellig* by David Almond (Hachette Children's Group, 2013)

- *Carrie's War* by Nina Bawden (Little, Brown Book Group, 2017)

- *Hacker* by Malorie Blackman (Corgi Children's, 2011)

- *The Boy in the Striped Pyjamas* by John Boyne (Penguin Random House Children's UK, 2014)

- *Cogheart* by Peter Bunzl (Usborne Publishing Ltd, 2016)

- *Letters from the Lighthouse* by Emma Carroll (Faber & Faber, 2017)

- *Just William* by Richmal Crompton (Pan Macmillan, 2015)

- *The Witches* by Roald Dahl (Penguin Random House Children's UK, 2016)

- *The Miraculous Journey of Edward Tulane* by Kate DiCamillo (Walker Books Ltd, 2008)

- *The London Eye Mystery* by Siobhan Dowd (Penguin Random House Children's UK, 2016)

- *When the Sky Falls* by Phil Earle (Andersen Press Ltd, 2021)

- *The Graveyard Book* by Neil Gaiman (Bloomsbury Publishing PLC, 2009)

- *The Weirdstone of Brisingamen* by Alan Garner (HarperCollins Publishers, 2010)

- *SilverFin* by Charlie Higson (Penguin Random House Children's UK, 2012)

- *The Phantom Tollbooth* by Norton Juster (HarperCollins Publishers, 2008)

- *The Jungle Book* by Rudyard Kipling (Penguin Random House Children's UK, 2013)

- *From the Mixed-Up Files of Mrs Basil E Frankweiler* by EL Konigsburg (Pushkin Children's Books, 2015)

- *The Nowhere Emporium* by Ross Mackenzie (Floris Books, 2015)

- *Goodnight Mister Tom* by Michelle Magorian (Penguin Random House Children's UK, 2014)

- *The Girl of Ink & Stars* by Kiran Millwood Hargrave (Chicken House Ltd, 2016)

- *The Midnight Guardians* by Ross Montgomery (Walker Books Ltd, 2020)

- *Kensuke's Kingdom* by Michael Morpurgo (HarperCollins Publishers, 2017)

- *The Phoenix and the Carpet* by Edith Nesbit (Little, Brown Book Group, 2017)

- *The Knife of Never Letting Go* by Patrick Ness (Walker Books Ltd, 2018)

- *Wonder* by RJ Palacio (Penguin Random House Children's UK, 2013)

- *Over the Line* by Tom Palmer (Barrington Stoke Ltd, 2016)

- *Wolf Brother* by Michelle Paver (Hachette Children's Group, 2011)

- *Tom's Midnight Garden* by Philippa Pearce (Oxford University Press, 2015)

- *The Brilliant World of Tom Gates* by Liz Pichon (Scholastic, 2019)

- *The Wolf Wilder* by Katherine Rundell (Bloomsbury Publishing PLC, 2020)

- *Holes* by Louis Sachar (Bloomsbury Publishing PLC, 2015)

- *There's a Boy in the Girls' Bathroom* by Louis Sachar (Bloomsbury Publishing PLC, 2016)

- *The Invention of Hugo Cabret* by Brian Selznick (Scholastic, 2007)

- *Black Beauty* by Anna Sewell (Penguin Random House Children's UK, 2012)

- *Treasure Island* by Robert Louis Stevenson (Penguin Random House Children's UK, 2008)

- *Around the World in Eighty Days* by Jules Verne (Independent Publishing Corporation, 2013)

- *The Murder's Ape* by Jakob Wegelius (Pushkin Children's Books, 2018)

- *Charlotte's Web* by EB White (Penguin Random House Children's UK, 2014)

Series

- *The Wolves Chronicles* series by Joan Aiken (Penguin Random House Children's UK, 2016)

- *Noughts + Crosses* series by Malorie Blackman (Penguin Random House Children's UK, 2017)

- *The Princess Diaries* series by Meg Cabot (Pan Macmillan, 2015)

- *Artemis Fowl* series by Eoin Colfer (Penguin Random House Children's UK, 2002)

- *Alex Rider* series by Anthony Horowitz (Walker Books Ltd, 2015)

- *The Roman Mysteries* series by Caroline Lawrence (Hachette Children's Group, 2002)

- *The Chronicles of Narnia* series by CS Lewis (HarperCollins Publishers, 2001)

- *Children of the Red King* series by Jenny Nimmo (Egmont UK Ltd, 2002)

- *His Dark Materials* series by Philip Pullman (Scholastic, 2019)

- *Percy Jackson* series by Rick Riordan (Penguin Random House Children's UK, 2013)

- *Harry Potter* series by JK Rowling (Bloomsbury Publishing PLC, 2014)

- *A Series of Unfortunate Events* series by Lemony Snicket (HarperCollins Publishers, 2012)

Classic fiction

Be aware that some of these books may be included in your child's secondary school English syllabus, so check in advance if possible.

- *Little Women* by Louisa May Alcott (Penguin Books Ltd, 2018)

- *Jane Eyre* by Charlotte Brontë (Penguin Books Ltd, 2006)

- *The Lost World* by Sir Arthur Conan Doyle (Penguin Random House Children's UK, 2019)

- *Just William* by Richmal Crompton (Pan Macmillan, 2015)

- *Robinson Crusoe* by Daniel Defoe (Penguin Books Ltd, 2012)

- *Great Expectations* by Charles Dickens (Penguin Books Ltd, 2003)

- *Oliver Twist* by Charles Dickens (Penguin Books Ltd, 2003)

- *Lord of the Flies* by William Golding (Faber & Faber, 1997)

- *The Secret Garden* by Frances Hodgson Burnett (Vintage Publishing, 2012)

- *The Jungle Book* by Rudyard Kipling (Penguin Random House Children's UK, 2013)

- *To Kill a Mockingbird* by Harper Lee (Vintage Publishing, 2015)

- *Goodnight Mister Tom* by Michelle Magorian (Penguin Random House Children's UK, 2014)

- *The Phoenix and the Carpet* by Edith Nesbit (Vintage Publishing, 2017)

- *Animal Farm* by George Orwell (Penguin Books Ltd, 2018)

- *Black Beauty* by Anna Sewell (Penguin Random House Children's UK, 2012)

- *The Adventures of Tom Sawyer* by Mark Twain (Penguin Random House Children's UK, 2008)

- *Around the World in Eighty Days* by Jules Verne (Independent Publishing Corporation, 2013)

- *The Sword in the Stone* by TH White (HarperCollins Publishers, 2008)

Fiction for advanced readers

- *The Diary of a Young Girl* by Anne Frank (Penguin Books Ltd, 2012)

- *A Little History of the World* by EH Gombrich (Yale University Press, 2008)

- *The Curious Incident of the Dog in the Night-time* by Mark Haddon (Vintage Publishing, 2004)

- *George's Secret Key to the Universe* by Lucy and Stephen Hawking with Christophe Galfard (Penguin Random House Children's UK, 2008)

- *Journey to the River Sea* by Eva Ibbotson (Pan Macmillan, 2021)

- *Emil and the Detectives* by Erich Kästner (Vintage Publishing, 2012)

- *The Earthsea Cycle* series by Ursula K Le Guin (Simon & Schuster, 2004)

- *Life of Pi* by Yann Martel (Canongate Books Ltd, 2018)

- *A Beautiful Lie* by Irfan Master (Bloomsbury Publishing PLC, 2011)

- *Trash* by Andy Mulligan (Penguin Random House Children's UK, 2014)

- *Five Children and It* by Edith Nesbit (Faber & Faber, 2014)

- *The Silver Sword* by Ian Serraillier (Penguin Random House Children's UK, 2015)

- *The Hobbit* by JRR Tolkien (HarperCollins Publishers, 1996)

- *The Book Thief* by Markus Zusak (Transworld Publishers Ltd, 2016)

Illustrated factual books

- *A Day in the Life of a Poo, a Gnu and You* by Mike Barfield and Jess Bradley (Michael O'Mara Books Ltd, 2020)

- *Knowledge Encyclopedia Space!: The Universe as You've Never Seen it Before* by Dorling Kindersley (Dorling Kindersley Ltd, 2021)

- *Shackleton's Journey* by William Grill (Flying Eye Books, 2014)

- *See Inside How Things Work* by Conrad Mason (Usborne Publishing Ltd, 2009)

- *The Bacteria Book: Gross Germs, Vile Viruses, and Funky Fungi* by Steve Mould (Dorling Kindersley Ltd, 2018)

- *How To Be Extraordinary* by Rashmi Sirdeshpande and Annabel Tempest (Penguin Random House Children's UK, 2019)

- *The Big Book of the Blue* by Yuval Zommer (Thames & Hudson Ltd, 2018)

Diary-style books

- *Iguana Boy Saves the World With a Triple Cheese Pizza* by James Bishop (Hachette Children's Group, 2018)

- *Mayhem Mission* by Burhana Islam (Knights Of Media, 2021)

- *The Extremely Embarrassing Life of Lottie Brooks* by Katie Kirby (Penguin Random House Children's UK, 2021)

- *Planet Stan* by Elaine Wickson (Oxford University Press, 2018)

Comic fiction

- *Cosmic* by Frank Cottrell-Boyce (Pan Macmillan, 2019)

- *The Spy Who Loved School Dinners* by Pamela Butchart (Nosy Crow Ltd, 2014)

- *Who Let the Gods Out?* by Maz Evans (Chicken House Ltd, 2017)

- *The Brilliant World of Tom Gates* by Liz Pinchon (Scholastic, 2019)

Graphic novels

- *The Fantastic Flying Books of Mr Morris Lessmore* by WE Joyce (Atheneum Books for Young Readers, 2012)

- *Hilda and the Troll* by Luke Pearson (Flying Eye Books, 2015)

- *Greek Myths* by Marcia Williams (Walker Books Ltd, 2006)

- *Malala's Magic Pencil* by Malala Yousafzai (Penguin Random House Children's UK, 2019)

Dyslexia-friendly fiction

- *Featherlight* by Peter Bunzl (Barrington Stoke Ltd, 2021)

- *Be Nice to Aunt Emma* by Anne Fine (Barrington Stoke Ltd, 2021)

- *D-Day Dog* by Tom Palmer (Barrington Stoke Ltd, 2019)

- *The Invasion of Crooked Oak* by Dan Smith (Barrington Stoke Ltd, 2020)

Magazines

- *Anorak* (Studio Anorak)

- *Aquila* (New Leaf Publishing)

- *The Caterpillar* (The Moth)

- *Kookie* (Missprint Media Limited)

- *The Loop* (Bolt Editions)

- *National Geographic Kids* (National Geographic Society)

- *Scoop* (C. Arthur Pearson Ltd)

- *The Week Junior* (Future Publishing Limited)

Wellbeing resources

Websites

BBC Bitesize Parents' Toolkit – The BBC website offers wellbeing resources for families, including tips, expert advice and fun activities to help parents support their child's wellbeing and learning in a changing world.

Parents' Toolkit (BBC Bitesize, 2021) www.bbc.co.uk /bitesize/articles/znsmxyc

CAMHS Resources – This site pools together various resources that are designed to support the mental health and wellbeing of young people and their parents or carers. The site offers lots of information on the places you can go for support with specific mental health challenges, from anxiety to special educational needs, eating disorders, depression, self-harm, bullying, and more.

CAMHS Resources, www.camhs-resources.co.uk

MindEd – MindEd is an online learning resource for anyone interested in the mental health of children and teenagers. It includes in-depth content on wellbeing and resilience, bereavement and loss, stress, trauma, anxiety, low mood, and more.

MindEd Hub (NHS Health Education England, 2021) www.minded.org.uk

Young Minds – Young Minds is the UK's leading charity committed to improving the emotional wellbeing and mental health of children and young people. Their website is full of fantastic resources for both parents and children, from advice on everything from supporting students through school transitions to helping children stay mentally healthy during exam season. There is also lots of great advice for parents dealing with specific mental health challenges their children have.

YoungMinds, www.youngminds.org.uk

Apps

Calm – Calm uses meditation techniques to aid with stress and sleep.

Happify – Happify turns the latest innovations in the science of happiness into activities and games, to help you lead a more fulfilling life.

HappiMe – HappiMe is a free app designed to raise self-esteem, self-confidence and happiness levels in children and young people.

Chill Panda – Chill Panda helps children better understand their stress and shows them ways to feel better using breathing techniques, yoga, exercise and calming games.

Combined Minds – This app was developed to help families and friends support young people with their mental health.

Feeling Good Teens – This app uses short audio tracks to help let go of worry, improve sleep, develop self-esteem, resilience and goal-focussed motivation.

Headspace – This is a popular meditation app. Meditation can be helpful for reducing stress and anxiety, enhancing focus and concentration and improving sleep.

Mindshift – Mindshift is a free app designed to help teens and young adults cope with anxiety.

Smiling Mind – This is a meditation programme developed by psychologists and educators to help bring mindfulness into your life.

What's Up – This app uses CBT methods to help users cope with depression, anxiety, anger, stress, and more.

Books

Children's Worry Book by Children's Mindfulness (CreateSpace Independent Publishing Platform, 2018) is a 'worry journal', designed to help children aged six to twelve document and manage their thoughts and feelings in a fun and accessible way.

The Unworry Book by Alice James (Usborne Publishing Ltd, 2019) provides an 'unworry toolkit' full of activities to help children manage their mood, such as creating a worry box, making a mood grid, and colouring, doodling and mazes.

Calm – Mindfulness for Kids by Wynne Kinder (DK Children, 2019) offers an introduction to mindfulness and teaches children how to be more mindful in everyday life by using fun activities.

Don't Worry, Be Happy by Poppy O'Neill (Vie, 2018) is a practical guide for overcoming anxiety, designed for children aged seven to eleven.

You're A Star: A Child's Guide to Self-Esteem by Poppy O'Neill (Vie, 2018) is a practical guide that combines proven CBT methods used by child psychologists in schools with simple activities to help children aged seven to eleven improve their self-esteem.

My Hidden Chimp by Steve Peters (Studio Press, 2018) offers advice on how to help children develop healthy habits for life.

Parenting Toolbox by Lisa Phifer, Laura Sibbald and Jennifer Roden (PESI Publishing & Media, 2018) is filled with easy-to-use strategies to overcome challenges and strengthen parent–child interaction, one worksheet, activity and exercise at a time.

Think Good – Feel Good by Paul Stallord (Wiley, 2018) is a CBT workbook designed to help young people to cope with low mood and anxiety.

Mindful Kids by Whitney Stewart (Barefoot Books, 2017) provides a card deck filled with creative games and exercises to help children practise mindfulness in everyday life.

My Anxious Mind by Michael A Tompkins (Magination Press, 2009) helps teens manage their anxious feelings using CBT strategies and helps them to feel more confident and empowered in the process.

The Author

 Mary Lonsdale is the CEO and founder of Mentor Education. For almost forty years, Mentor has offered professional one-to-one tuition in London and worldwide, helping over 90,000 children achieve top grades, gain entry to the best schools, and discover the joy of learning. Mary started her own education at Merchant Taylors' School for Girls and went on to study English and Classics at Leeds University.

Mary grew up in a household of teachers and so has always understood the value and importance of education. It was this that inspired her to found Mentor Education, where the company's touchstones are a professional yet personal service and a compassionate, holistic approach. More than just improving grades or passing exams, Mentor aims to have a positive impact on every child they teach and to ignite a lifelong love of learning. Mary's passion for education is the driving force behind Mentor and motivates her desire to help as many children as possible achieve their full potential.

🌐 https://mentoreducation.co.uk

🅕 www.facebook.com/mentoreducationuk

🐦 https://twitter.com/MentorEdUK

🅘 www.instagram.com/mentoreducationuk

Printed in Great Britain
by Amazon

15545208R00122